Manager Selection

Statement of Purpose

The Research Foundation of CFA Institute is a not-for-profit organization established to promote the development and dissemination of relevant research for investment practitioners worldwide.

Editorial Staff

Nicole R. Lee
Book Editor

David L. Hess
Associate Editor

Cindy Maisannes
Manager, Publications Production

Randy Carila
Publishing Technology Specialist

Biography

Scott D. Stewart, CFA, is a member of the board of directors of the Boston Security Analysts Society. Between 2002 and 2012, he was a research associate professor in the finance department at the Boston University School of Management and the faculty director of the Master of Science in Investment Management program. Dr. Stewart joined Boston University after a career in portfolio management that included global equity, fixed-income, and asset allocation investing in mutual fund, separate account, and commingled pool formats. He has broad experience in both being selected as an investment manager and selecting managers to help implement his strategies. His investment career included 14 years at Fidelity Investments, where he was founder and equity group leader of the $45 billion Structured Investments Group. He managed the active Fidelity Fifty Fund, Fidelity Select Equity Portfolios, Fidelity Funds America, and the Perpetual America Fund and co-managed the Fidelity Freedom Funds, earning recognition for superior investment performance from Micropal, the *Wall Street Journal*, and *Barron's*. He introduced Fidelity's indexed equity mutual funds in 1988 and managed the first issue during its inception year. Dr. Stewart was also senior adviser to equity research at Fidelity and a portfolio manager at State Street Bank Asset Management Division (now State Street Global Advisors), where he managed both active and indexed fixed-income assets, active tactical asset allocation portfolios, derivative strategies, and indexed equities. His research interests include portfolio management techniques, the behavior of institutional investors, equity valuation, the use of technology in finance, and management education. He speaks at both academic and practitioner conferences, has published articles in the *Financial Analysts Journal*, the *Journal of Portfolio Management*, and the *Financial Review*, and has served as an ad hoc reviewer for each of these publications. He is associate editor of the *Journal of Risk Finance* and co-author of *Running Money: Professional Portfolio Management* (McGraw-Hill, 2010). Dr. Stewart actively manages money, consults, and teaches investment research and portfolio management. He earned an MBA and a PhD in finance at Cornell University.

Contents

Foreword

For more than a half century, a great deal of thought and effort has gone into methods for identifying desirable securities (see Graham and Dodd 1934) and efficiently combining them into portfolios that maximize expected return for a given amount of risk (see Markowitz 1952). But today, as in the past, most investors do not select securities themselves; they select managers—either institutional investment managers or mutual fund managers—to select securities for them. The art and science of selecting managers has received less attention than that of selecting securities, but it is important in today's world and deserves at least the attention given to it in this book.

There are two threads of prior work on manager selection. The first thread, which is by far the larger one, is the literature that asks whether it is possible for fund managers to beat the market, whether they actually do so, whether they earn alphas bigger than their fees, and whether the alpha is repeatable or predictable. If alpha is predictable, then one can select superior managers in a manner analogous to Graham and Dodd's quest for superior securities. The second thread asks, in the spirit of Markowitz, what is the best way to combine managers to build an overall portfolio that maximizes risk-adjusted return?

Can Managers Beat the Market and Earn Positive Alphas?

Sharpe (1991) examined the philosophical question of whether managers in aggregate can beat the market. If the managers' holdings sum to those of the market, their aggregate return before costs must equal that of the market. After costs, the aggregate of manager returns must be less than the market return. This principle is a mathematical truth, does not depend on circumstances, and applies to all asset classes (not just equities). Sharpe (1992) later identified common factors—value, growth, large capitalization, and small capitalization—that explain fund returns and that can be used both to categorize funds and to measure alpha after an adjustment for a fund's factor exposures.

Do Managers Earn Positive Alphas? Are They Repeatable?

Although the whole population of managers cannot be winners, some managers will beat the market or earn a positive alpha (that is, beat the relevant benchmark after an appropriate adjustment for risk). Whether they do so by luck or skill is an important area of ongoing investigation. The first scientific study of mutual fund returns was Jensen (1968), who found that "active mutual fund managers were unable to add value and, in fact, tended to underperform the market by approximately the amount of their added expenses" (Malkiel 2003, p. 77). Using more recent data, Malkiel (1995) confirmed Jensen's results. A number of researchers have found persistence in fund alphas, but Carhart (1997) found that "persistence in mutual fund performance is due to the use of simple momentum strategies by fund managers, rather than to certain managers having 'hot hands' that allow them to pick winning stocks" (Daniel, Grinblatt, Titman, and Wermers 1997, p. 1058).

The Goetzmann–Ibbotson series of "Do Winners Repeat?" studies is a major contribution to this thread and is generally less negative in its conclusions. Goetzmann and Ibbotson (1994), Brown, Goetzmann, and Ibbotson (1999), and Ibbotson and Patel (2002) found a winners-repeat effect in mutual funds, hedge funds, and other actively managed portfolios.

Finally, Siegel, Kroner, and Clifford (2001) took a different approach by studying the best managers, not the average manager. They asked, how good are the best managers? They found that 43 of the 494 funds studied had 20-year alphas in excess of 2% per year, providing a sense of scale to the claims of active managers. They also investigated what the best managers have in common and whether there are more of them than would occur at random. They found that the best managers had almost nothing in common and that there are more of them than would occur randomly even though they are rare.

How to Build Portfolios of Managers

Waring, Whitney, Pirone, and Castille (2000) and Waring and Siegel (2003) noted that building a portfolio of managers is similar to building a portfolio of anything: It is an optimization problem. The inputs required are the active return (expected alpha), expected active risk, and expected correlation of active returns. This work is an extension of the seminal treatise on quantitative active management by Grinold and Kahn (2000), which deals with optimization at the security selection level.

The problem with this method is that most investors do not have much confidence in their manager-specific alpha forecasts. The authors would argue that this lack of confidence bolsters the case for indexing, but most investors build the majority of their "portfolios" with active managers anyway.

This Book

Stewart, a professor at Boston University and former portfolio manager at Fidelity Investments, synthesizes the various threads that I mentioned earlier.

He begins with advice on process and structure, a focus that anyone who has managed money will recognize as vitally important. Chapter 2 discusses identifying skilled active managers and builds on the observation that most investors, including those aware of the zero-sum arithmetic of active investing, seek out such managers. The next chapter deals with indexing. In the spirit of the Waring articles referenced earlier, Stewart's Chapter 5 addresses the combination of active and index managers in the same portfolio. Chapter 6 covers performance measurement and related activities, and Chapter 7 reveals recent research findings. In chapter 8, Stewart provides assistance to the underserved community of financial advisers. The remainder of the book addresses alternative investments and draws general conclusions.

Investors who allocate capital to managers, rather than selecting securities themselves, have become an important, if not dominant, force in the markets. The Research Foundation of CFA Institute is delighted to present this book to aid them in their efforts.

Laurence B. Siegel
Gary P. Brinson Director of Research
CFA Institute Research Foundation

REFERENCES

Brown, Stephen J., William N. Goetzmann, and Roger G. Ibbotson. 1999. "Offshore Hedge Funds: Survival and Performance 1989–1995." *Journal of Business*, vol. 72, no. 1 (January):91–117.

Carhart, Mark M. 1997. "On Persistence in Mutual Fund Performance." *Journal of Finance*, vol. 52, no. 1 (March):57–82.

Daniel, Kent, Mark Grinblatt, Sheridan Titman, and Russ Wermers. 1997. "Measuring Mutual Fund Performance with Characteristic-Based Benchmarks." *Journal of Finance*, vol. 52, no. 3 (July):1035–1058.

Goetzmann, William N., and Roger G. Ibbotson. 1994. "Do Winners Repeat? Patterns in Mutual Fund Behavior." *Journal of Portfolio Management*, vol. 20, no. 2 (Winter):9–18.

Graham, Benjamin, and David Dodd. 1934. *Security Analysis*. Burlington, NC: American Media International.

Grinold, Richard C., and Ronald N. Kahn. 2000. *Active Portfolio Management*. 2nd ed. New York City: McGraw-Hill.

Ibbotson, Roger G., and Amita K. Patel. 2002. "Do Winners Repeat with Style?" Yale International Center for Finance Working Paper 00-70 (February).

Jensen, Michael C. 1968. "The Performance of Mutual Funds in the Period 1945–1964." *Journal of Finance*, vol. 23, no. 2 (May):389–416.

Malkiel, Burton G. 1995. "Returns from Investing in Equity Mutual Funds: 1971–1991." *Journal of Finance*, vol. 50, no. 2 (June):549–572.

———. 2003. "The Efficient Market Hypothesis and Its Critics." *Journal of Economic Perspectives*, vol. 17, no. 1 (Winter):59–82.

Markowitz, Harry. 1952. "Portfolio Selection." *Journal of Finance*, vol. 7, no. 1 (March):77–91.

Sharpe, William F. 1991. "The Arithmetic of Active Management." *Financial Analysts Journal*, vol. 47, no. 1 (January/February):7–9.

———. 1992. "Asset Allocation: Management Style and Performance Measurement." *Journal of Portfolio Management*, vol. 18, no. 2 (Winter):7–19.

Siegel, Laurence B., Kenneth F. Kroner, and Scott W. Clifford. 2001. "The Greatest Return Stories Ever Told." *Journal of Investing*, vol. 10, no. 2 (Summer):91–102.

Waring, M. Barton, and Laurence B. Siegel. 2003. "The Dimensions of Active Management." *Journal of Portfolio Management*, vol. 29, no. 3 (Spring):35–51.

Waring, M. Barton, Duane M. Whitney, John Pirone, and Charles Castille. 2000. "Optimizing Manager Structure and Budgeting Manager Risk." *Journal of Portfolio Management*, vol. 26, no. 3 (Summer):90–104.

Preface

Most investors delegate the responsibility of implementing their investment policy to portfolio managers. Developing an effective manager selection process is critical to retaining highly skilled managers who maintain objectives consistent with those of the investor.

This book focuses on the task of manager selection from the perspective of institutional investors and includes insight and recommendations for financial advisers and individual investors alike. It was inspired by 30 years of experience as a portfolio manager, researcher, and fiduciary as well as by being on both sides of the manager selection process. In all three roles, I have studied the selection decisions of institutional investors and published recommendations relevant to industry practice.

I have drawn on research results and the experience of practitioners to provide a comprehensive tool for developing a rigorous process for manager selection. In this book, I discuss qualitative techniques and quantitative tools and also incorporate cases, reviews of empirical research, and Excel templates to illustrate recommended techniques.

Readers are encouraged to review this book in its entirety, but individual chapters may be referenced for specific topics. Chapter 1 highlights the influence of investment policy statements on the manager selection process, and Chapter 10 provides a summary of key recommendations. Investors planning to hire active, indexed, or alternative managers may want to reference Chapters 2, 3, and 9, and those hiring multiple managers may find Chapters 4 and 5 of interest. Chapter 6 presents techniques for monitoring current managers, and Chapter 7 documents empirical results of studies that test quantitative and qualitative methods for successful manager selection. Financial advisers and individual investors may be particularly interested in Chapter 8.

Writing this book has been a pleasure. I have enjoyed the opportunity to explore, study, and evaluate many fascinating techniques. I hope you find this helpful when hiring your next portfolio manager.

Acknowledgments

This book would not have been possible without the academic training, career opportunities, and learning experiences offered to me over the years by my family, teachers, supervisors, work associates, clients, and students. Thank you.

Laurence Siegel provided patient guidance on this project, and his insights and creative suggestions have helped with both the content and organization of this book. Nicole Lee and David Hess, in the editorial group at CFA Institute, also helped to make the book a success. The Research Foundation of CFA Institute generously provided financial support for the project. Thank you.

A number of people have contributed their time and frank perspectives, which helped me incorporate real-world points of view into the text. I thank Paul Brakke, Budge Collins, Charles Ellis, Kevin Ely, F. Douglas Foster, Eric Knutzen, Erik Molander, and Ronald Peyton.

And I would like to thank my wife, Pamela Morse Stewart, for her help editing this book. She has consistently shown patience with and support for this project and the other time commitments I have made over the years.

All errors remain mine.

1. Introduction

Why We Care about Manager Selection

Manager selection is a critical step in implementing any investment program. Investment objectives may be finalized and targets for asset class weights may be set, but an investment plan is not productive until it is implemented through the purchase or sale of securities, properties, commodities, or derivatives. Even professional investors rarely make all investment decisions on their own. In most cases, investors choose portfolio managers to determine the most appropriate instruments in which to place assets. Investors hire portfolio managers to act as their agents, and portfolio managers are trusted to perform to the best of their abilities and in investors' best interests.

Portfolio managers may be responsible for selecting individual securities, sectors, or asset classes. Tactical asset allocation managers, for example, actively weight assets and delegate to other managers the selection of individual securities. Hybrid quant–fundamental managers seek to consistently outperform benchmarks through active security selection. Index managers use advanced risk models and focus on efficient trading to deliver benchmark returns consistently, within a single basis point in some cases.

Investors can be individuals, pension plan sponsors, endowments, foundations, or corporate entities. Individuals saving for retirement, for example, commonly select mutual fund managers to invest their defined contribution savings. Pension plan sponsors often manage a portion of their assets in house, but they typically hire institutional managers to implement most mandates.

The task of manager selection involves more than simply picking active managers with a goal to outperform benchmarks. Investors must practice due diligence when selecting index managers as well as active portfolio managers. Investors want managers who are highly skilled, diligent, and persistent, but they also want managers whose interests are aligned with their own. And investors need to do more than identify skillful managers; they need to determine the appropriate weights to give these managers.

Institutional and retail investors have a poor record in conducting the manager selection process. Empirical research into the effectiveness of hire and fire decisions suggests that investors tend to hire managers and fire managers at the wrong times. Perhaps this finding is attributable to the tendency for investors to extrapolate returns and not be comfortable making decisions until after they wait for extended periods of superior performance to serve as "buy" signals, which may occur near the peaks of managers' performance cycles. It may also be related to a lack of understanding regarding manager beta, style, and extremeness of style exposures. A thorough understanding by investors of the challenge of finding and blending skillful managers should help improve the record. That is the goal of this book.

How Manager Selection Fits within the Investment Process

As noted earlier, manager selection is one of the final steps in developing and implementing a comprehensive investment plan. Investors typically begin by formulating an investment policy statement (IPS) that articulates their financial needs, philosophy, asset allocation policy, and expectations. At the implementation stage, a management agreement document that spells out benchmarks, expected returns, and acceptable risk levels is typically prepared for each mandate and manager. In some cases, such as limited partnership contracts or mutual fund prospectuses, the agreement is set by the manager (although a "side letter" listing special understandings with a specific client may be prepared). Manager objectives that are consistent with the investment needs and goals formulated in the IPS should be created. The overall process is summarized in **Exhibit 1.1.**

Exhibit 1.1.   The Investment Process: Step 1, Preparing the IPS

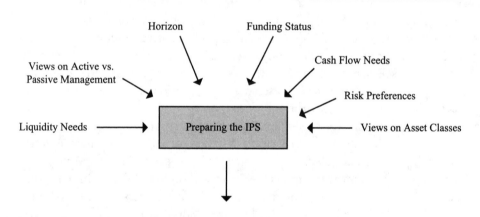

1. General Investor Description
2. Duties of Parties
3. Investment Objectives
    • Return Goals
    • Risk Tolerances
4. Liquidity, Timing, and Other Constraints
5. Benchmarks, Asset Allocation Ranges, and Acceptable Investment Management Styles, Vehicles, etc.
6. Guidelines for Review, Rebalancing, and Adjustments
7. Other Information

The IPS has important implications for manager selection. It should include background concepts and document the investment objectives that the investor considers most relevant in determining appropriate managers and setting relationship expectations. It should also include a description of the client or investor, the overall mission, and the goals and objectives for investing the assets. There may be a specific spending policy or time horizon that informs the decisions of setting the asset allocation and determining the style of underlying managers. For example, a client who wants to manage downside risk relative to a liability may seek options protection or conservative managers. Acceptable risk levels and liquidity needs should also be specifically documented in the IPS. For example, an investor who needs ready access to funds may want to avoid private equity mandates. **Exhibit 1.2** summarizes common features listed in IPS documents, including references for manager selection.

Implications of the Investment Policy Statement

Investors' views, horizons, sizes, and experiences influence the formulation of the IPS and, in turn, affect the manager selection process. Small investors are limited by their asset size to investing in mutual funds and exchange-traded funds (ETFs), medium-size investors may be able to access certain premier managers via intermediaries, and the largest, most well-connected investors may have direct access to premier hedge funds and private equity firms. In addition, large investors that want active management and access to all asset classes may also need to select multiple managers to be able to invest in capacity-constrained categories, such as small-cap equities, special situation real estate, and seed-capital venture funds.

Investors' liquidity needs and cash flow horizons will likewise influence the writing of the IPS and, in turn, the manager selection. Some investors have ongoing contributions and withdrawals. They need managers who offer both full market exposure and daily liquidity. Defined benefit pension plans have well-defined liabilities that tend to have durations longer than the overall bond market.[1] Such plans need fixed-income managers who are able to customize portfolios to effectively match those long durations.

The selection of appropriate asset classes and target weights directly affects the manager selection process. Restricting investment to the public markets (essentially the stock and bond markets) simplifies the process because of public pricing transparency. Holding broadly diversified

---

[1]Duration is the present-value-weighted average timing of cash flows, and it measures the sensitivity of an asset or liability's price to changes in interest rates or discount rates.

Exhibit 1.2. Various IPS Features and Their Implications for Manager Selection

IPS Features	Implications for Manager Selection
1. Client description	
Asset size	Investment vehicle, manager availability
Cash flow profile	Manager liquidity profile
Liability profile	Manager duration flexibility
2. Duties	
Responsibility for asset class selection	Complexity of manager process
Responsibility for defining manager guidelines	Complexity of management guidelines
Responsibility for manager selection	Complexity of manager process
Responsibility for negotiating fees	Complexity of fee structure and incentives
Responsibility for monitoring managers	Complexity of manager process
3. Objectives	
Return objectives	
Total vs. relative	Manager hedging ability
Real vs. nominal	Manager inflation-hedging ability
Risk objectives	Level of manager total and active risk
Fee/expense guidelines	Passive vs. active, availability of incentive fees
4. Constraints	
Liquidity	Manager liquidity policy
Horizon	Manager duration
Taxes	Tax management ability
Legal and regulatory	Vehicle, manager diversification
Investment restrictions	Management credit and derivative exposure
5. Asset allocation targets	
Asset class selection	Manager asset exposure
Acceptable styles	Manager process/Style exposure
Number of asset classes	Manager diversification
6. Guidelines for adjustment and rebalancing	
Frequency/rules	Manager liquidity
7. Schedule for reviews	
Frequency/access	Manager availability

portfolios of publicly traded stocks or bonds reduces the number of managers required to provide total portfolio diversification. Index funds are the best example of this approach. The addition of alternative asset classes to the asset mix and, consequently, to the IPS complicates the manager selection process. For example, investment staff need sufficient resources to handle the additional work load. Because alternative investment funds are commonly limited by time horizon and by the number of individual properties they include, investors in these funds need to seek many more managers than they would if they were using publicly traded securities to fulfill the same percentage allocation. They also need to be responsible for funding capital calls and reinvesting proceeds in new partnerships.

Real Story: Effort Required to Monitor External Managers

Consider the number of private equity managers retained by the Massachusetts Pension Reserves Investment Management Board (PRIM), a $41 billion state pension system, relative to public equity managers, shown in **Table 1.1**. More than 70% of the managers[2] selected were in private equity despite the fact that it represents only 10% of total assets.

Table 1.1. Manager Diversification by Asset Class

Asset Class	No. of Managers	Proportion of Managers	Target Allocation
	Pension Reserves Investment Trust Fund		
Public securities	17	12.1%	67%
Real estate	12	8.6	14
Economic targeted investments	8	5.7	1
Private equity	98	70.0	10
Hedge funds	5	3.6	8
Total	140	100.0%	100.0%

Source: PRIM (2010).

As prices and opportunities change, investors need to rebalance their portfolios to match target allocations. Larger asset sizes and tighter allocation bands require liquid vehicles to implement changes. Some custodian banks offer equity or fixed-income funds that use futures contracts to facilitate daily liquidity. Investors need to determine a process for evaluating these vehicles.

If investors assume responsibility for manager selection, contract negotiation, and monitoring but do not have the skill or time to fully understand and monitor the investment marketplace, they can increase the chance of meeting market-based performance goals by using index managers.

---

[2]Note that more than 200 individual partnerships were listed in the report.

It is unrealistic to assume that part-time or unsophisticated investors can analyze and select alternative asset or other active managers and succeed at identifying effective managers and capturing valuable alpha, especially without expert advice.

Many investors maintain an overall plan benchmark for the purpose of monitoring results versus objectives. Active performance can be attributed to individual decisions, including asset allocation, style allocation, and manager selection. Accurate performance attribution requires valid benchmarks. Many managers' investment styles are difficult to define by using common market-weighted indices and require more creative means to describe manager processes.

Derivatives can be used to transfer total returns (and alpha) from one asset class to another. For example, alpha generated from a zero-beta market-neutral strategy can be transported to other asset classes (i.e., to add value over an equity benchmark by using equity index futures contracts, at a cost). Some investors' liabilities will automatically rise with inflation, which will require the IPS and underlying managers to pursue real returns. The degree to which an investor prepares to make use of these investment capabilities will influence manager selection.

Some investors, such as those who seek protection of principal or constant purchasing parity, may not use a standard capitalization-weighted benchmark index. These investors may need to seek managers with derivatives capabilities and use option-protected benchmarks or inflation-adjusted indices.

Portfolio risk guidelines vary by type and level and may be highly customized. For example, some investors may be comfortable with close-tracking managers who limit the level of performance volatility around the managers' benchmarks. Others may wish to limit downside, requiring their managers to offer option-like features in their portfolios. These guidelines need to be incorporated in the IPS and, as a result, will restrict the list of acceptable managers to those who will control portfolio risk.

Real Story: Looking at a Sample IPS

Exhibit 1.3 illustrates that investors need to develop a view on manager selection prior to defining the IPS. The University of California Retirement Plan is a $35 billion defined benefit plan for public university employees of the state of California. Its IPS documents the many details that influence the types of managers it hires. Its investment objectives refer to benchmarks, restrictions, and expectations for communication.

Exhibit 1.3. Selected Text from a Sample IPS: Implications for Manager Selection

Sample Text from University of California Retirement Plan

Section	Text
Objectives	
2. Investment Policy	"Capital Market . . . Asset Class . . . Manager Value-Added Risk"
	"[Manager] risk is an implementation risk and is the responsibility of the Treasurer (and indirectly the investment managers)."
	"select managers with experience and expertise . . . benchmark and range of probable outcomes"
4. Performance Objectives	"Return should exceed the Consumer Price Index on a consistent basis over time."
	"Return should match or exceed the total Retirement Fund weighted benchmark return."
	"Leverage may be used in Private Equity, Real Estate, and Absolute Return strategies."
5. Asset Class and Manager Guidelines	"All individual manager guidelines will be consistent with broad asset class guidelines and this Policy."
Appendix	"several risk measures which focus on surplus risk . . . [and] ratio of plan assets to liabilities"
	"Active risk or 'tracking error'"
Constraints	
2. Investment Policy	"implement procedures to provide efficient management of liquidity"
5. Asset Class and Manager Guidelines	"The purchase of securities issued by tobacco companies is prohibited in separately managed accounts."
	"The use of derivative securities or contracts to create economic leverage in the portfolio is prohibited."
Appendix	US Equity: Russell 3000 Tobacco Free Index
Rebalancing	
Appendix	"monitor monthly . . . rebalance assets . . . in a timely and cost effective manner when actual weights are outside the prescribed ranges"
	"may utilize derivative contracts (in accordance with Appendix 4) to rebalance the portfolio"
Schedule for Reviews	
5. Asset Class and Manager Guidelines	"Managers are required to submit periodic reports to the Treasurer summarizing investment activity and strategy."
	"Managers are required to reconcile investment returns with the custodian each month."

Source: May 2006 University of California Retirement Plan Investment Policy Statement.

Most investors recognize the importance of seeking high returns net of fees and understand that higher net returns may require higher management fees. But because fees are easy to measure and returns are hard to forecast, some investors include specific guidelines in their IPSs on fee levels and structures. Low fee requirements lead investors to seek index, low-alpha, and high-capacity managers. IPS guidelines may also include explicit requirements for incentive fees, thus making it necessary to find managers who offer flexibility in structuring fee formulas.

The rigidity of investment constraints clearly influences the appropriateness of particular managers. Investors who need liquidity may be restricted from using real estate or private equity limited partnerships. These investors can provide for some liquidity in their portfolios and invest in these asset classes by using real estate investment trusts (REITs), which are publicly traded real estate securities, and a basket of publicly traded private equity firms. As the financial market turmoil in late 2008 illustrated, liquidity becomes more important and less readily available during periods of market stress. In fact, in early 2009, investors tried to privately sell their shares in limited partnerships at a significant discount to valuations prepared only months earlier. Particular time horizon constraints, such as the timing of liability cash flows, will inform the choice of appropriate investment styles and managers. Short-term cash flow needs will limit an investor's flexibility to use volatile or illiquid vehicles despite the potential for high returns.

Individual investors, corporate entities, and foundations are all subject to taxes in one form or another. Individual investors must pay national and local taxes on interest, dividends, and capital gains and may be limited in their ability to deduct losses. Corporate investors are also subject to income and capital gains taxes but have more flexibility in using losses to reduce taxable income. Charitable foundations, tax free to a large extent, may be subject to particular features of the US tax code, such as UBIT (unrelated business income tax). High-turnover managers who do not consider the effects of capital gains realization may not be appropriate for investors who will be taxed. Many investors select tax-efficient equity managers, tax-advantaged bond managers (such as municipal bond managers in the United States), or high-dividend managers (those who take advantage of the corporate dividend exclusion in the US tax code). In some cases, limited partnership structures, including offshore entities, are formed to limit tax exposures.

Many IPS documents limit investments to high-quality issues, such as investment-grade bonds. The goal is to limit the chance of a default and a significant loss of principal. Fixed-income mandates, for example, may restrict managers from purchasing individual bonds with Standard & Poor's ratings below BBB. These guidelines disqualify certain types of managers and, thereby, impact the terms of the manager agreement. For example, the manager agreement may allow a manager to keep issues that have been downgraded, or conversely, it may require the manager (along with many other holders) to sell the issues as soon as a downgrade is published. If the manager is required to do the latter, credit research capabilities become a very important criterion for manager selection.

Some investors restrict the purchase of particular classes of securities or securities in the domicile or industry of the issuer. This restriction may be related to social policy guidelines, religious restrictions, or other diversification factors. Consider the example of eliminating securities of companies that sell tobacco or alcohol. This approach may require the elimination of an individual manager or an entire class of managers, or it may require choosing a manager who can provide a separately managed account that follows a customized strategy.

The inappropriate or naive application of options, futures, swaps, and structured products has led to the current situation in which derivatives are considered too risky for most market participants. To the uninformed, these instruments can yield surprising performance results. Used wisely, they can provide valuable hedging benefits with limited credit risk.[3] Because of the high-stakes complexity of using some derivatives, many investors prefer to avoid them altogether and include such restrictions in their IPSs. Others allow them to a limited extent. They are hard to avoid entirely; consider the common use of US Treasury bond futures by fixed-income managers to control portfolio durations. Investors who are comfortable with derivatives should ensure any managers using them are well qualified as part of the manager search process.

Using leverage, like derivatives, can also lead to unpleasant surprises. But many managers, including hedge fund, private equity, and real estate portfolio managers, commonly use it. Investors should specify their comfort level with leverage vehicles in the IPS. If leverage and derivatives are both objectionable investment techniques, the set of acceptable, talented managers will be limited.[4]

Academicians and practitioners alike have extensively explored the value of active management. Research on the efficient market hypothesis and the record of active managers suggests, at a minimum, that adding value consistently on a statistically significant, risk-adjusted basis is a remarkable achievement.[5] In spite of this challenge, a large majority of assets are managed actively. Investors need to do many things right to be successful: identify

---

[3]One approach is to explore what may happen to the provider when the markets are under pressure. For example, consider when the insurance will be needed and when the provider will be at risk of going bankrupt.

[4]Note that the issuers of many individual securities use leverage in their regular business activities.

[5]Note that the market does not have to be efficient for active management to be difficult. Active management is a zero-sum game, so no matter how inefficient the market, about half of all active managers will lose money (relative to the benchmark, when properly risk adjusted) before costs. This subject is explored in Chapter 2.

managers with a high probability of adding value, select an attractive time to invest with those managers, and continuously monitor and decide when to terminate them. Active management requires manager diversification to limit the risk of the overall portfolio underperforming its benchmark. This extra layer of diversification, in turn, requires more effort.

Using active managers requires investors to engage in ongoing monitoring activity. Many active managers, such as hedge fund managers, are uncomfortable sharing information on their trades and underlying holdings. Others happily display their positions on a regular basis. Some funds—for example, "1940 Act" mutual funds—offered to the general public in the United States are required to publish their holdings. In any case, investors who seek to actively monitor risk in their total portfolios will need access to, or at least estimates or summary risk measures of, their underlying positions. Those who firmly require this information will need to hire managers who are comfortable sharing it.

Investment Implementation

Once the investment policy statement has been prepared and target asset allocation weights have been defined, the assets are put to work. A summary of the steps for implementing the investment decision is provided in **Exhibit 1.4**.

As discussed earlier, asset allocation policy is articulated in the IPS, and target weights, combined with asset size and preferences, have a direct influence on the number of managers needed to implement the investment plan. Multiple managers may be needed to diversify active management, whereas one or two index managers may be acceptable to fulfill an asset class assignment. Tax status may also influence the number of managers. After-tax performance is typically more efficient if generated within a single portfolio where changing security characteristics do not force the sale of issues, particularly those with unrealized capital gains. Multiple portfolios require effective trade coordination and sharing of tax lot information across managers who cannot anticipate future gain realizations from other portfolios. As illustrated in Table 1.1, the use of alternative investments, including limited partnership vehicles, will expand the number of managers and complicate the effort required for implementation, including selection, monitoring, meeting capital calls, and reinvesting proceeds.

Manager Selection

The scope of the selection process depends on the type of manager being sought. For example, the number of searches, the depth of inquiry, and the intensity of monitoring during the process are very different for index versus active managers, as well as for public market versus private market active managers. Factors to consider and questions to ask may be informed by the summary of key manager decisions and characteristics listed in **Exhibit 1.5**. The categorization is

Exhibit 1.4.   The Investment Process: Step 2, Implementation

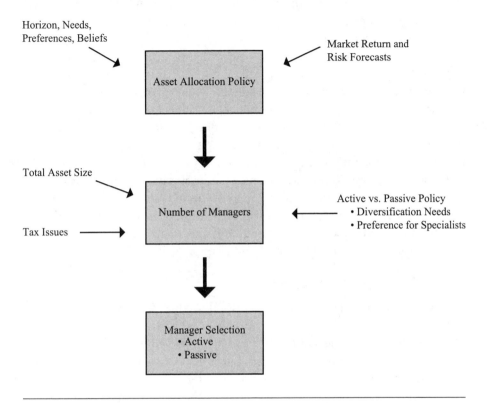

Exhibit 1.5.   The Investment Process: Implementation, Manager Selection

	Three Portfolio Management Processes	
Index	Active Public Investments	Active Private Investments
Key manager decisions		
Diversification	Buy and sell decisions	Buy and sell decisions
Trading costs	Diversification	Management of underlying properties
Cash management		Diversification
Key account characteristics		
Pooled or segregated account	Pooled or segregated account	Limited partnership structure
Easy to terminate	Easy to terminate	Difficult to terminate

more complex than the table suggests. For example, a hedge fund manager may use liquid, publicly traded securities even though the fund's limited partnership structure may make it cumbersome to redeem the investment.

Investors hire managers as their agents to construct and maintain portfolios, pay management fees, and hold managers accountable for performance. The managers offer expertise to investors and assume responsibility for real-time monitoring and trading.

Investors seek capable managers who will apply their skills and diligence to the role, but it is not easy to measure skill and diligence or to determine whether they will persist once identified. Many investors rely heavily on reported performance track records, which are subject to cyclicality. As documented by empirical research, investors tend to hire active managers near the peaks of their cycles, leading to disappointing subsequent performance. Index investors may not fully understand the process for tracking a benchmark by using sampling techniques and thus may not know the right questions to ask. Because investment management is a complicated process, many investors seek help in the form of financial advisers, pension or investment consultants, and fund-of-funds managers. Outsourcing the manager selection decision creates an additional hiring decision and layer of agency.

Organization of This Book

This introduction to manager selection is followed, in Chapter 2, by the topic of active management. As previously discussed, the investor's view on the use of active managers influences the IPS and its implementation. A full indexing approach may be simple and low risk, but it also restricts exposures to asset classes and may result in an inferior risk–return balance.

Chapter 3 reviews the index fund management process, as well as strategies for tracking benchmarks, and concludes with a list of key questions for investors to ask prospective managers. Asset allocation techniques and their implications for manager selection are reviewed in Chapter 4, which also documents how manager selection decisions and asset class policies are interrelated. For example, because managers may have biases correlated with asset classes and alphas can be correlated across managers, there is a trade-off involved when selecting the manager with the highest potential and accepting underlying portfolio biases. Investors will not be able to simultaneously meet asset class policy goals and retain their favorite managers without conflicts between these two objectives.

Chapter 5 begins with an integrated discussion of active and index management and describes several techniques for combining managers, in addition to demonstrating the use of Microsoft Excel in building optimizers to help set manager weights. Chapter 6 reviews the dynamics of manager selection, including monitoring, performance analysis, and fee incentives. In the last 10 years, researchers have begun to study the behavior of institutional investors when making manager selection decisions and have documented the performance impact of these decisions. Individual investors have been the subject of academic research for many years. Chapter 7 summarizes the results for both groups, providing evidence to inform the manager selection process.

Financial advisers are responsible for small institutional investors and individual investors, including both high-net-worth and other individuals. Relative to traditional institutional investors, individual clients are less sophisticated and are responsible for lower asset levels, but they are demanding nonetheless. Chapter 8 reviews manager selection issues for financial advisers, including tax strategies. Although all the chapters include non-US and non-traditional investment examples for discussion, Chapter 9 is specially dedicated to manager selection issues for global markets and alternative asset classes. Chapter 10 concludes with summaries of best practices and key recommendations.

2. Identifying Skilled Active Managers

The Arithmetic of Active Management

If we gather the returns of all securities that are publicly traded in a security market in a given time period and weight them by their value outstanding at the beginning of the period, we will have a measure of the return of that market for that period. If we gather the returns of all portfolios—both indexed and active, institutional and retail—and weight them by their value, the calculation (before fees and transaction costs) will yield the same number—the return on the market. If all the portfolios are not identical in composition, some will exhibit performance that is higher than the market and some will exhibit lower performance. But on average—when the weighted average return is calculated—the portfolio returns will equal the market return.[6]

A key element to consider in this analysis is transaction costs. Market averages typically include only closing prices. Returns calculated from these will not reflect any costs incurred in purchasing the securities. Transaction costs may include commissions, bid–ask spreads, and market impact (widening of spreads with increasing order size). Live portfolios do experience these costs, and as a result, their returns, on average, will be lower than the return on the market.[7] Index funds, which trade less frequently than active funds, are affected to a lesser degree by transaction costs.

Sharpe (1991) summarized these observations in two distinct statements.[8] Assuming a world where each manager can own only the index constituents, the index funds (frequently called passive managers) and active managers own all the outstanding issues in the index, and the averages are weighted according to portfolio asset size, Sharpe stated that

> (1) before costs, the return on the average actively managed dollar will equal the return on the average passively managed dollar and (2) after costs, the return on the average actively managed dollar will be less than the return on the average passively managed dollar. (p. 7)

The first statement follows from computing the sum of asset-weighted returns in an assumed closed universe. The second statement is the result of system leakage to brokers and dealers at a higher level of costs for active managers

---

[6]Appendix A shows this argument expressed in mathematical terms.
[7]Some portfolios seek to boost returns by providing liquidity to the market, offsetting the drag of costs on the portfolio but not the average.
[8]An analysis by D. Umstead, distributed by State Street Bank & Trust Co. in 1985, makes a similar point.

than for index managers attributable to higher levels of trading. Several conclusions follow, as long as the arithmetic assumptions hold in the real world:

- Active managers, as a group, cannot outperform market index funds.

- If transaction costs are not too high and active managers are sufficiently different from the representative index funds, some managers will outperform.

- In order for some active managers to outperform, others must underperform.

This principle of outperformance can be illustrated by assuming a normal probability distribution of manager returns distributed symmetrically around the equal-weighted mean manager return with some variance. Because the funds' asset values differ, the value-weighted and equal-weighted means would not necessarily equal each other.[9] But if the dataset is comprehensive (including all holders, including individuals), the asset-weighted mean return of all managers before costs and excluding influence from cash (and other non-index) positions will equal the market index return. **Figure 2.1** illuminates the fact that for some managers to outperform, some must underperform.

Figure 2.1.   Illustration of the Arithmetic of Active Management Assuming Normal Cross-Sectional Distribution of Manager Returns

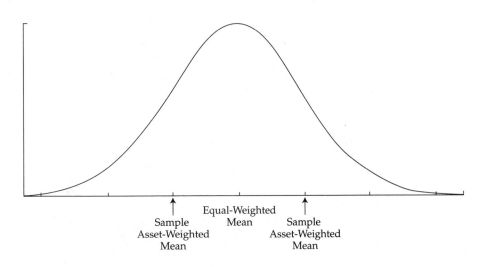

[9]See Appendix A for more detail.

15

Evidence on the Arithmetic

Empirical evidence supports these conclusions. But as Sharpe noted, one must apply his proposition with care and not uncritically accept published data that purport to prove that active managers as a group either out- or underperform the market. For example, before computing these numbers for analysis, it is important to note that all the data needed to compute the portfolio averages may not be publicly available. The value of the market return and the computed average portfolio return are not necessarily identical in light of the fact that the value and return of some portfolios (or portion of portfolios) are simply not observable. Consider, for example, stocks held by individual investors either in a brokerage account or in the form of paper certificates[10] or shares trading in one country's market that are held in part by investors as a portion of an overseas portfolio.[11] As a result, the two figures will not necessarily match. One must also be careful to avoid excluding poorly performing portfolios that have dropped out of a performance database. This survivorship bias will artificially increase the performance of a published universe of managers.

The US equity mutual fund market has been studied extensively and provides a large sample of actively managed and indexed portfolios for examination. **Table 2.1** illustrates some of the empirical issues involved in measuring the arithmetic of active management. It includes both equal- and value-weighted mean manager returns, before and after adjusting for survivorship bias, relative to an index fund and two market indices.

Table 2.1. Sample Calculations of the Arithmetic of Active Management: Mean Annual Portfolio Returns, 1977–1988

	Mean
Equal-weighted managers	14.5%
Value-weighted managers	13.6
Survivors only, value weighted	13.8
S&P 500 Index mutual fund	13.2
S&P 500 Index	14.0
Wilshire 5000 Index	14.7

Note: The sample includes all publicly offered, open-ended, common stock mutual funds offered in the United States.
Source: Brown and Goetzmann (1995).

[10]In 1997, 60% of exchange-listed US equities were owned by individual investors, and in 2005, 35% were (Agarwal 2007).

[11]In 2007, the value of overseas holdings of US equities totaled $3.13 trillion (Forbes 2010). Although some of these assets may be listed in publicly available US institutional manager databases (if managed in separate accounts by US managers), this figure represents 20.7% of the value of shares listed on the NYSE and NASDAQ.

The table shows that equal- and value-weighted means and narrow and broad market indices can differ markedly, even over 10-year horizons. Over this particular period, small-cap stocks outperformed large caps (the Wilshire 5000 includes small- and mid-cap stocks whereas the S&P 500 excludes them) and active managers had a tendency to hold small- and mid-cap stocks to a greater extent than that reflected in market-cap-weighted indices. See the following box for a full discussion of the importance of cap-size differences.

Focus: Looking at the Averages

If the return on the average fund does not always equal the return on the market, where are the missing portfolios? As an example, consider returns on the average large-cap US equity mutual fund and the S&P 500. **Figure 2.2** plots the difference in 12-month returns between the average of the Lipper large-cap growth and value universes and the S&P 500. Lipper publishes returns of mutual fund "indices" or equal-weighted mutual fund returns based on various classifications. Despite focusing on only the US equity large-cap funds for analysis, returns vary between the two series by more than 2% in almost half of the periods.

Figure 2.2.   Difference in 12-Month Returns: S&P 500 Index minus Large-Cap Mutual Funds, 1989–2008

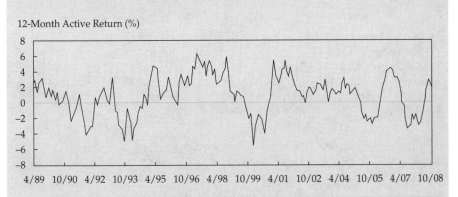

Note: Data are from the Lipper large-cap growth and large-cap value mutual fund series.
Source: Based on data from Lipper Analytical Services.

There are two things going on here. First, the average portfolio is not the same as the universe of portfolios. The latter is asset weighted and should more closely reflect the total market as defined by a capitalization-weighted index. Second, active managers, on average, tend to hold smaller-cap stocks at larger weights than do market-cap-weighted index funds.

For further analysis, I considered all the holdings of US equity mutual funds offered in the US market[12] and computed financial characteristics and sector weights relative to the S&P 500. This information for both equal- and asset-weighted schemes is displayed in **Table 2.2**.

Table 2.2.   Portfolio Characteristics of Equal- and Asset-Weighted US Equity Mutual Fund Portfolios and the S&P 500, 30 June 2012

	Equal-Weighted Funds	Asset-Weighted Funds	S&P 500
Market capitalization ($ millions)			
Weighted average	$72,931.3	$97,954.0	$110,453.7
Median	470.3	470.3	12,024.3
Weighted median	20,045.0	40,203.2	56,082.4
Dividend yield	1.80%	1.94%	2.09%
P/E: Weighted harmonic average	15.6	15.0	14.5
P/E using FY1 est.: Weighted harmonic average	14.0	13.5	13.0
P/E using FY2 est.: Weighted harmonic average	12.4	12.0	11.6
Price/book: Weighted harmonic average	2.1	2.2	2.1
Price/sales: Weighted harmonic average	1.3	1.3	1.3
Historic three-year sales growth	11.0%	10.4%	8.0%
Historic three-year EPS growth	16.6	16.0	14.3
Estimated three- to five-year EPS growth	12.4	11.8	10.9

Sources: Based on data from Capital IQ and FactSet.

The table shows that the asset-weighted universe of mutual funds is more similar to the market-cap-weighted S&P 500 than the equal-weighted average, as is reflected in the two sets of fund characteristics. The average mutual fund is smaller in market capitalization than the asset-weighted average, which, in turn, is smaller than the S&P 500 average. Consistent with the small-cap bias, the average fund has a lower dividend yield, a higher P/E, and higher earnings and sales growth rates. The asset-weighted results indicate that larger-asset funds hold large-cap stocks in greater weights.

---

[12]The holdings include all mutual funds located in the United States with at least 90% of holdings in US equities listed in the Capital IQ database (3,408 as of June 2012).

©2013 The Research Foundation of CFA Institute

The market-cap distribution of the average mutual fund can be explored further by sorting holdings by their market capitalizations and comparing the weightings of the stocks for the average mutual fund and the S&P 500, as illustrated in **Figure 2.3**.

Figure 2.3. Market Capitalizations and Portfolio Weights of Holdings in the Average US Equity Mutual Fund and the S&P 500, 30 June 2012

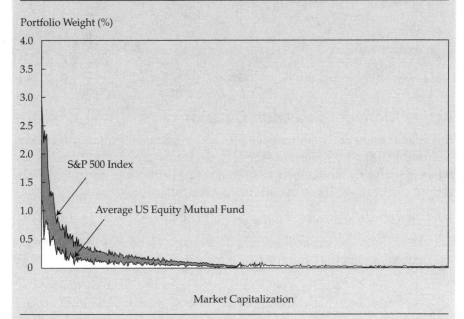

Source: Based on data from Capital IQ.

Figure 2.3 indicates that in a given period, the average mutual fund holds less of its weight in the largest-market-cap names than the cap-weighted S&P 500 does and the excess portfolio weight is invested in a long tail of smaller-cap stocks than are represented in the S&P 500. In addition to holding more small-cap stocks, the managers weight many names more heavily than market weighting would require.

These results suggest that the return on the average mutual fund relative to the S&P 500 will be influenced by the differences in performance of small- and large-cap stocks. **Table 2.3** summarizes the performance differences of the underlying holdings of equal-weighted and asset-weighted aggregations of US equity mutual funds for July 2012. Note that the Wilshire 4500 Index is composed of small- and mid-cap stocks. In conclusion, any measure of active managers' performance must be adjusted for differences in characteristics between their portfolios and the benchmark index. Alpha estimates that use market, style, and fundamental factor risk models help address this issue.[13]

Table 2.3. Average Performance of Securities Held in US Equity Mutual Funds: Equal- and Asset-Weighted Holdings vs. S&P 500 and Wilshire 4500, July 2012

Holdings or Index	Performance
Holdings of mutual funds, equal weighted	0.72%
Holdings of mutual funds, asset weighted	1.12
S&P 500	1.39
Wilshire 4500	−0.68

Sources: Based on data from Capital IQ and FactSet.

Active Manager Selection Decision

Investors need to develop their views on active management prior to crafting an investment policy statement. The IPS specifies acceptable investments and types of managers in addition to overall investment goals. To justify hiring active managers, the investor must believe the following:

1. Some portfolio managers have the skill to deliver superior performance.

2. The investor has the skill to identify managers who will deliver superior performance in the future.

3. The investor can build a portfolio of managers to effectively deliver asset class exposure as specified in the IPS and capture superior performance after costs.

As previously mentioned, academicians and practitioners alike continue to investigate the value of active management. Research on the efficient market hypothesis, the arithmetic of active management, and the performance record of investors' past active manager selections suggests, at a minimum, that effectively adding value on an after-cost, risk-adjusted basis is a significant challenge. In spite of this challenge, a majority of assets—even in high-visibility, large-cap, publicly traded equities—are managed actively. **Table 2.4** shows that as of 2008, more than 80% of US mutual fund assets are actively managed.

Incorporating the option for active management broadens the challenge of implementing the investment policy. Investors need to do many things right to be successful. They must identify a manager with a high probability

---

[13]Three- and four-factor models, such as those of Fama and French (1993) and Carhart (1997), are estimated linearly and may not pick up the full influence of varying market caps. For an example of this issue, see Stewart (2013).

of adding value, select an attractive time to invest with that manager, continuously monitor the portfolio, and decide whether and when to terminate the manager. Active management requires manager diversification to limit the risk of underperforming benchmarks. This requirement demands additional effort on the part of investors. Not surprisingly, many investors seek the assistance of a pension consultant or financial adviser for help with this process.

Table 2.4. Assets under Management for ETFs and Active and Indexed US Equity Mutual Funds

	No. of Funds	Billions of Dollars under Management	Proportion of Dollars under Management
Indexed	336	751	11.5%
ETFs	547	545	8.4
Active	3,884	5,226	80.1
Total	4,767	6,521	100.0%

Source: ICI (2008).

Modern portfolio theory (MPT) is used to help explain the price of risk by expressing quantitatively the benefits of diversification, the existence of nondiversifiable (systematic) risk, and the level of return an investor requires to hold risky assets. The return on a security or portfolio of securities is related to its exposure to market factors, which, in turn, vary based on changes in the business cycle, interest rates, technological developments, and so forth. The single-factor capital asset pricing model (CAPM) articulates the relationship between portfolio risk and expected return in the following equation:

$$E(R_P) = R_f + \beta_P \left[E(R_M) - R_f \right], \tag{1}$$

where

E = expectations operator

R_P = portfolio return

R_M = market return

R_f = risk-free return

β_P = sensitivity of the portfolio return to the market return

Although this model includes some unrealistic assumptions,[14] such as the irrelevance of transaction costs, it is a very useful tool for formulating one's view regarding the manager selection process. For example, the CAPM shows that a portfolio's expected return is related to expected market returns. It also shows that the return at any given time is determined, in part, by how

---

[14]Standard investment textbooks, such as those by Sharpe, Alexander, and Bailey (1999) and Bodie, Kane, and Marcus (2010), review these assumptions.

sensitive the portfolio is to the market (the β, or beta term). Investors looking for higher expected returns can simply increase their exposure (including leverage) to the overall market.[15]

This initial equation does not address the potential to add value through active management. In the model expressed by Equation 1, expected portfolio return is determined solely by a risk-free rate and a constant linear exposure to an expected market return. The CAPM *model* does not allow for manager alpha. In other words, a nonzero alpha is not compatible with CAPM assumptions. But the CAPM *equation* can be easily modified to represent an actively managed portfolio, as illustrated in the following equation:

$$E(R_P) = \alpha_P + R_f + \beta_P \left[E(R_M) - R_f \right], \tag{2}$$

where

α = excess return from active management (alpha)

Note that an index fund should have zero alpha, but a portfolio with zero alpha may not necessarily be an index fund; zero alpha is also consistent with a given manager having no skill. In this model, skill is defined by the exhibition of positive alpha. **Figure 2.4** illustrates this relationship wherein the security market line shows the trade-off between expected return and beta. Portfolios A and C exhibit betas greater than 1, and Portfolios B and C exhibit alphas less than 0.

Figure 2.4. The Security Market Line with Sample Portfolios

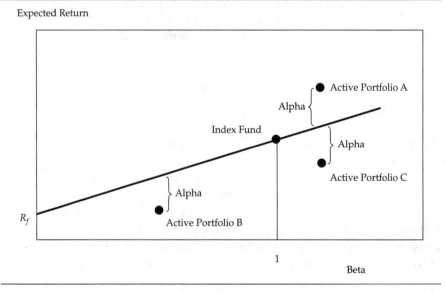

[15]A higher expected return does not necessarily mean a higher realized return.

22
©2013 The Research Foundation of CFA Institute

It is important to note that the asset-weighted beta of all portfolios in the market must sum to one. Although alpha may be positive for a single skillful manager, the arithmetic of active management requires that the positive alpha be balanced by the existence of a manager with negative alpha. Alpha must total zero for all managers when all managers are combined on an asset-weighted basis.[16] In other words, the total dollar alpha[17] must sum to zero.

The concept of market efficiency has relevance when exploring active management. The efficient market hypothesis (EMH) states that currently available information is reflected in current security prices and that investors cannot effectively profit from this information. If this hypothesis is true, then the alpha for every manager (not just managers in aggregate) is zero and any realized alpha in practice is attributable to an inaccurate risk measurement or simply noise (random variation that is not related to true skill). In the latter case, the appearance of some highly successful active managers may be related to the fact that given any set of random numbers, probability dictates that some will appear at the top of the ranking. Jarrow (2010)[18] noted that a constant alpha from a single strategy is highly unlikely because it would be consistent with the existence of a persistent arbitrage opportunity, which is rare. What is believed to be true alpha may instead be the result of an unobservable market factor. Jarrow further stated that investors evaluating an active manager should "understand the market imperfection that is causing the arbitrage opportunity" (p. 21) and be able to identify the market participants who are losing money in the process.

There are different forms of the EMH, each of which relates to the definition of market information. The "weak form" proposes that price trends and reversals are simply random events with no serial correlation and, therefore, one cannot profit from studying past patterns, such as historical volume and price data. (The weak form does not say that studying company fundamentals is useless.) The "semi-strong form" proposes that new financial information is reflected in security prices too quickly to result in profits. The "strong form" proposes that even nonpublic data, such as insider information, is incorporated into security prices.

---

[16]The total is before transaction costs and fees and excludes portfolio cash positions.

[17]The total is before transaction costs and fees and excludes portfolio cash positions.

[18]He noted that market complexities suggest that market disequilibriums are not uncommon but a persistent opportunity would be rare. An insurance policy on an event that does not occur in a given time period is one example of an unobservable factor creating the appearance of alpha. An insider-trading scheme, as long as it persists, is an example of a constant alpha. Its success would require a loser (consistent with the arithmetic argument).

The question is whether the EMH holds true in live markets. In the real world, there is a cost for collecting information. Some participants are willing to pay costs if profitable arbitrage conditions (inefficiencies) exist. This willingness to pay costs moves prices closer to true values. Grossman and Stiglitz (1980) explored the pricing of securities using a mathematical model that considers both arbitrage opportunities and costs, as well as informed and uninformed investors. They concluded that market prices do not fully reflect underlying asset values, with the difference between the two depending on the level of costs, the number of informed investors, and the amount of noise in the system. In other words, prices do not reflect all publicly available information, and investors who operate with low costs can profit by trading on this inefficiency.

Evidence relevant to the EMH suggests that it is difficult to generate positive alpha by identifying market inefficiencies, particularly in large-cap US equities. The presence of apparent inefficiencies may be attributable to misspecified risk models. Consider, for example, small-cap, P/E, and momentum effects.[19] Evidence of anomalies, documented behavioral tendencies of investors, and the apparent persistence of realized alpha suggest that markets may not be fully efficient and some managers can generate superior returns, even in the US equity market.

Measurement of Active Manager Alpha

Equation 2 expresses a model of expected (*ex ante*) portfolio return determined by market returns and risk, plus a factor for manager excess return greater than that explained by risk. Empirical evidence indicates that the CAPM beta model explains approximately one-third of actual (*ex post*) individual stock return variance. Multifactor models that incorporate beta risk measures of sector exposures, company size, market valuation, growth measures, and price momentum explain more. Yet, even a fully developed model cannot explain all returns; there is always a degree of noise in the data that cannot be explained in every period. To convert the aforementioned expressions to realized returns for a particular period of time, time subscripts and an error term must be added, as illustrated in the following equation:

$$R_{Pt} = \alpha_P + R_{ft} + \beta_P \left(R_{Mt} - R_{ft} \right) + e_t, \qquad (3)$$

where

e_t = unexplained return in period t

---

[19]The average excess performance of small-cap stocks can be addressed with a market-cap risk factor, but the return pattern (with the excess return of small caps over large caps predominantly in the first two weeks of January) and nonlinear tendencies require a more complicated solution.

The expected value of the error term is zero and is assumed to be independent of the market return. This equation is commonly referred to as Jensen's alpha model,[20] and in practice, the single-factor equation (Equation 3) is estimated using linear (ordinary least-squares) regression techniques. The regression slope is beta and the intercept is alpha, both of which are constants.[21]

For convenience, the alpha and error terms can be combined into a single measure called "theta."[22] This term is a random variable, not correlated with the market. Its expected value is alpha. The CAPM assumes theta has an expected value of zero.

Statistical regression is a valuable technique to determine whether a given manager has delivered excess returns over a given period of time, adjusted for his or her specific average beta exposure to the market. Statistical techniques can be used to test for the significance of the alpha.

The arithmetic of active management, tested with the averages summarized in Table 2.1, can be retested by using alpha measures designed to adjust for benchmark mismatches, such as differences between the S&P 500 and the Wilshire 5000. In addition to the single-factor model described earlier, it is common to study performance by using three risk factors (market, valuation, and size) or four risk factors (price momentum is the fourth). Average alphas for US equity mutual funds are presented in **Table 2.5**.

Although this technique is more sophisticated than computing averages of active returns, a similar conclusion is reached. Asset-weighted average gross (before fees) risk-adjusted active returns (alphas) are not statistically different from zero using all three models. In other words, on average, active US equity mutual

Table 2.5. Average Gross Alphas for Active Equity Managers Based on One-, Three-, and Four-Factor Regression Estimates for US Equity Mutual Funds, 1984–2006

	Single Factor	Three Factor	Four Factor
Equal-weighted alpha[a]	0.18	0.36	0.39
t-Statistic	0.31	0.85	0.90
Value-weighted alpha[a]	−0.18	0.13	−0.05
t-Statistic	−0.49	0.40	−0.15

[a]Percent gross alpha, 12 × monthly average.
Source: Fama and French (2010).

---

[20]See Jensen (1968) as well as any investment text.
[21]Recall that the beta regression coefficient equals the covariance of the portfolio and market returns divided by the variance of the market return.
[22]See Grinold and Kahn (2000). Many practitioners refer to theta and alpha interchangeably, but readers should be wary of this practice, as they should be of any convention that confuses expected and realized values of a variable.

fund managers do not generate a positive alpha, even gross of expenses. Note that expenses would detract between 94 bps and 131 bps annually from performance.

Although equity mutual funds do not, on average, generate alpha, especially net of fees, equity managers hired by large institutional investors have earned positive alphas on an equal-weighted basis using one- and three-factor models. Busse, Goyal, and Wahal (2010) took an approach similar to that of Fama and French (2010); their results are summarized in **Table 2.6**. Note that management fees would detract roughly 50 bps annually from performance.

Table 2.6. Average Gross Alphas for Active Equity Managers Based on One-, Three-, and Four-Factor Regression Estimates for Institutional US Equity Managers, 1991–2008

	Single Factor	Three Factor	Four Factor
Equal-weighted alpha[a]	2.28	1.40	0.80
t-Statistic	3.17	2.52	1.34
Value-weighted alpha[a]	0.52	–0.04	0.20
t-Statistic	1.06	–0.05	0.40

[a]Percent gross alpha, 4 × quarterly average.
Source: Busse et al. (2010).

Evidence of Active Manager Alpha

The arithmetic of active management demonstrates that (gross) portfolio alphas should equal zero on an asset-weighted basis. It also illustrates that some managers may outperform or underperform market averages. It does not indicate, however, that some portfolio managers have the skill to deliver superior performance. The EMH questions whether any managers have the ability to create alpha. In other words, in the theory's strongest form, true alpha for all managers equals zero. Using the EMH as a reference, it is important to determine whether some managers exhibit skill with high statistical confidence. If some do, investors can explore whether it is worthwhile to seek the group that will outperform. Their efforts should include documenting management fees as well as transaction, search, and monitoring costs.

Given a large sample of managers, it should not be difficult to find some with performance records that suggest statistically significant alphas. But this assumption ignores the fact that the best managers were cherry-picked from the sample. For a fair test, it is important to recognize that over time with a large set of managers distributed randomly, the probability that there will be some unusually high and unusually low performers is 100%. A better test can be conducted: one that compares the real world with a world of randomness to determine whether the number of high-alpha managers is statistically different from what one would expect in the absence of skill. This test should adjust for the fact that a set of observed managers is smaller than the universe of all managers. Studying multi-factor risk-adjusted alpha estimates instead of total returns will help in this task.

Based on such a test, it appears the answer is yes: Skillful managers do exist. But the number of managers that demonstrate, with high statistical confidence, that they have skill may be small. Research based on US equity mutual funds—arguably one of the most challenging universes in which to add value—suggests that unusually strong or weak results are attributable not to luck but rather to skill or negative skill.

Fama and French (2010) reviewed the distribution of active manager performance and compared it with a random distribution of zero-mean alphas to determine statistically whether over- and underperforming managers deliver results from the application of skill or simply based on luck.[23] Their tests suggest that more managers generate high levels of statistically significant risk-adjusted performance than randomness alone would suggest and, similarly, that more managers generate statistically low levels of alpha than would be expected from luck.

Table 2.7 summarizes these results, listing *t*-statistics of alphas computed over a 22-year period for groups of managers, sorted by computed *t*-statistics and compared with a distribution of *t*-statistics from a randomized world with variable but zero alphas. The alphas are listed in the form of *t*-statistics, rather than raw alphas, to standardize for variability through time. A positive number in the third column of Table 2.7 indicates that a group outperformed the simulated results; the top 10% and top 5% of the sample have positive numbers in this column, which provides evidence that those groups added value. To summarize, the top and bottom 10% of mutual fund managers have

Table 2.7. *t*-Statistics of Alphas for Percentile Ranges of Actual vs. Simulated Zero-Alpha Managers, 1984–2006

Performance Percentile for Fund	*t*-Statistic for Actual	*t*-Statistic for Simulation	Difference
Bottom 5%	−2.1	−1.7	−0.4
Bottom 10%	−1.6	−1.3	−0.3
Bottom 40%	−0.3	−0.3	0.0
Top 40%	0.3	0.3	0.0
Top 10%	1.6	1.3	0.3
Top 5%	2.1	1.7	0.4

Note: *t*-Statistics are based on monthly time series of regression-estimated, four-factor, gross-of-expenses alphas for US equity mutual funds.
Source: Fama and French (2010).

---

[23]The randomly generated return series are computed from 10,000 Monte Carlo simulations using alpha standard deviations estimated from historical results and zero-mean alphas.

generated gross alphas higher and lower, respectively, than simple randomness in a population would suggest. The test results indicate that there is skill in the tail deciles, gross of expenses. But there is little evidence to indicate there is sufficient statistically significant alpha to cover expenses.

Busse et al.'s (2010) analysis of institutional manager performance provides similar conclusions regarding the top 5% and 10% of managers. If this pattern is present in other markets and asset classes, a search for alpha, or at least exploring that potential, is justified.

Impact of Transaction Costs and Asset Size on Alpha Potential

There are costs associated with implementing any investment policy. They include the cost of hiring a new manager as well as costs a manager incurs when trading securities to maintain exposures or capture alpha. Transaction costs include commissions, bid–ask spreads, and market impact. Market impact refers to expanding bid–ask spreads with increasing order size for a given time period. As the asset size in a given strategy expands, so does the market impact to execute trades, which reduces portfolio returns. The size of this reduction depends on the liquidity (trading volume is one measure) of the portfolio's underlying securities, the strategy's turnover rate, the portfolio's number of holdings, and, for an active strategy, the reduction in alpha if the manager must supplement positions with less attractive holdings. Transaction costs can be reduced by extending the time it takes to complete a trade, but even if other market participants do not profit from observing the trade, delays will increase the risk that prices move in a significantly negative direction. It is important to recognize that market conditions affect transaction costs and, in turn, alpha potential. If markets are under stress, volumes may decline and bid–ask spreads may expand, which makes it difficult to implement actively traded strategies.

A strategy's capacity depends on turnover, transaction cost functions of its underlying positions, and decisions made by the manager regarding acceptable alpha. For protection, an investor should have a clear understanding of the manager's policy regarding capacity limits. If managers want to protect their clients' interests and their own reputations by limiting the impact of asset size on performance,[24] they should assess the costs of implementing their strategies and set a maximum level of assets to manage. Hopefully, this cap will be acceptable to all. Because it is difficult to forecast capacity, conservative managers tend to set intermediate or temporary limits that they will not exceed prior to a period of evaluation. In recent decades, markets may have become more efficient, but trading volume has increased by such a large extent that capacity has increased as well.

---

[24]Vangelisti (2006) called such limits "threshold capacities."

Selecting Managers with Positive Alpha

On average, active managers do not exhibit skill, nor should they because as a group, they approximate the market average. In fact, the EMH questions whether any manager exhibits skill. But empirical evidence suggests that skill does exist for the top 10% of managers in the US equity markets, which is one of the most efficient markets in the world. This finding suggests that a search for alpha is not unreasonable. But can investors identify skillful managers, in advance of hiring them, to profit from positive alpha? In other words, once positive-alpha managers are identified, do their alphas persist?

If positive alphas persist over time, investors should be able to collect historical returns, compute alphas, and select a set of managers with the highest performance. Regrettably, although evidence suggests this approach works in the short term, the alpha appears to decay over time. Two key observations regarding the characteristics of alpha create complications for its measurement:

1. Alphas seem to vary over time for individual managers (i.e., alpha itself exhibits randomness or at least cyclicality).

2. Alphas are not normally distributed cross-sectionally (across managers over a given period in time) or, for many managers, serially (over time for a given manager).

Focus: The Chance of at Least One Manager Exhibiting Good Performance

It is commonly believed that superior managers exist.[25] But if skill is measured by simply using past investment returns, can it be determined whether superior performance is the result of skill or luck? How can one tell with confidence whether an individual manager demonstrates skill within a population of many active managers?

The probability that there will be one portfolio manager in a given universe who will outperform all others is 1.0. Simply looking at past results for a population of funds does not prove that the top performers earned their rank through skill. Based on statistical analysis, their rank may or may not be a result of skill. Some manager will end up on top either by exhibiting true skill or by success attributable to noise (random variation) with zero true alpha. Consider a population of 1,000 managers, each with an annual residual risk of 5%. If we assume managers exhibit zero alpha and that residual risk is normally distributed and independent of the market, approximately 25 managers will generate a return of 10% above and 25 will generate a return of 10% below the average alpha. There will be one or two managers whose performance is 15% above the average—an economically

---

[25]See Siegel, Kroner, and Clifford (2001).

huge performance advantage. Even if it is assumed that returns in excess of the market are not serially correlated, as time extends past one year, it is expected that the top manager's cumulative performance will be higher than 15% above average. If some managers exhibit risk greater than 5%, there is a greater probability that they will end up at the top (and bottom), even when their true expected alpha is zero.

Standard statistical techniques can be applied to test for the significance of a given manager's record, but to be applied correctly, as pointed out by Baks, Metrick, and Wachter (2001), the method used for picking the manager must be taken into account. If the manager is selected at random, a simple *t*-test (assuming no survivorship bias) can be used to examine whether the alpha is greater than zero at a given confidence level. But if the manager is picked after sorting the universe of managers by performance, a single *t*-test is not appropriate. The test must be modified to determine the probability that at least one manager in the sample could have generated a given *t*-statistic value simply by luck.

Table 2.8 illustrates the importance of the sample size for determining with high statistical confidence whether a manager generated positive alpha. The significance of a *t*-test calculated from the best-performing manager's performance (10 years of monthly data is assumed in the table) ranges from a 100% chance of observing at least one *t*-value of 2.0 attributable to luck in a universe of 1,000 managers to a 0.0% chance of seeing a *t*-value of 5.0 attributable to luck in a universe of 10 managers.

Table 2.8.   Probability of Observing a Given Manager *t*-Statistic Assuming Zero True Alpha for Varying Sample Sizes and 120 Observations

| | *t*-Statistic | | | |
No. of managers	2.0	3.0	4.0	5.0
10	38.7%	3.2%	0.1%	0.0%
100	99.3	28.1	1.1	0.0
1,000	100.0	96.3	10.5	0.2

Note: Probability = $[1 - (1 - t\text{-Test } p\text{-value})^{No. \, of \, managers}]$.

Fama and French (2010) and Kosowski, Timmermann, Wermers, and White (2006) both tested whether skill exists in the population of active mutual funds. They examined all managers' returns and noted that the tails of manager gross performance are greater than expected simply because of randomness. This finding suggests that groups of managers have exhibited true skill.

Kosowski et al. (2006) studied the performance of US equity mutual fund managers and determined, after modifying statistical tests for nonnormality, that top managers do produce significant alphas. They also found, with statistical confidence, that alphas estimated over 36 months persist in the subsequent year, although they deteriorate from one period to the next. These findings are illustrated in **Table 2.9**.

Table 2.9. Persistence of Alpha from One Year to the Next in US Equity Mutual Funds, 1975–2002

	Net Alpha	Gross Alpha
All managers	−0.4%	0.5%
Top-decile managers[a]	3.6	4.6
Top decile, subsequent year[b]	1.0	1.9

[a]Calculated as 12 × Monthly alpha.
[b]Estimated from published expense ratios.
Note: Alpha was calculated by using regression estimates of four-factor alphas.
Source: Kosowski et al. (2006).

An earlier study by Stewart (1998) using a separate dataset and nonparametric techniques yielded similar results. He determined that ranking institutional US equity managers by historical frequencies of quarterly active returns was successful in identifying future superior managers over subsequent periods of three and five years. In contrast, there was no predictive power in ranking managers solely by active returns.

Although these findings validate the technique of selecting active managers by extrapolating evidence of past superior returns, the use of these techniques does not guarantee success. For example, based on the values found in Table 2.9 and the associated study's published parameter estimates, the probability of capturing a gross alpha of at least 100 bps in a given year by hiring five recent top-decile managers is approximately 65%. Net of fees, the probability drops to 50%. Choosing more than five funds diversifies risk and improves the odds of success.

Barras, Scaillet, and Wermers (2010) also sought to separate skill from luck when studying manager alphas in US mutual fund data and tested ways to capture future positive alpha. For the period 1979–2006, they reported a declining percentage of skillful managers as the number of total funds grew dramatically.[26] They demonstrated a technique that included estimating both the number of skillful managers through time

[26]Researchers noted a similar pattern in the hedge fund universe, which is reviewed later in this book.

and a measure of luck for each manager. They then applied both estimates to annual manager rankings. This selection technique has been shown to be superior to ranking managers solely by historical returns, alphas, or *t*-statistics.

Strategies to select managers on the basis of historical alphas often incur costs beyond management fees and expense ratios. Additional costs include the time it takes to collect data, conduct statistical analyses, and enter orders. Clearly, successfully capturing added value by selecting skillful managers is a challenge.

Qualities of Successful Managers

Can the odds of realizing positive alphas be improved in ways other than by hiring many managers, and are there particular characteristics associated with skillful managers? Professional investors have strong opinions regarding which qualities a good manager should have. For example, Buffett (2001) seeks a high energy level, basic intelligence, and high ethical standards when selecting professionals to manage Berkshire Hathaway businesses. Treynor (1990) proposed the importance of two factors: advanced knowledge of investments and a keen focus on the investment process. Talented investors must also love to learn. They persistently seek new information about the latest technologies, economic developments, and market sentiment. Swensen (2000) explained the importance of long-term thinking and individually driven decision making in generating superior performance. He stressed that a close alignment of interests between the manager and the client is a key requirement for future success. A summary of Buffett's, Treynor's, and Swensen's key characteristics of successful managers are listed in **Exhibit 2.1**.

Exhibit 2.1.	Key Characteristics of Successful Investment Managers
	Factor
1	Intelligence
2	Knowledge
3	Focus
4	Long-term thinking
5	Independent thinking
6	Alignment of interests

Sources: Buffett (2001); Treynor (1990); Swensen (2000).

These characteristics should be reviewed in the due diligence process, which is often called an analysis of people, philosophy, and process[27] and is carried out by sophisticated investors or pension consultants. The goal of due diligence is to confirm that an investment organization has the expertise to deliver superior performance. Due diligence includes questioning the source of added value and exploring how the manager is going to capture that source within a diversified, live portfolio, after costs. It also includes studying staff training and experience. There is still no guarantee that a manager who satisfies an investor's due diligence criteria will have superior performance, but it is a good start.

Quantifiable, Qualitative Characteristics of Good Investment Managers

Some may ask whether there is a way to quantify largely qualitative characteristics in a systematic review of prospective managers. In addition, is there any evidence that searching for these characteristics offers any value?

The key characteristics of successful managers outlined in Exhibit 2.1 can be measured in many ways. The factor of basic intelligence can be measured using IQ tests, standardized aptitude exams, and school grades. Knowledge can be evaluated by considering years of schooling, the conferment of advanced degrees, the length and type of work experience, certifications, and scores on achievement tests. Ability to focus and the degree of focus are difficult to measure but can be proxied by the number of hours in an individual's work week. The degree of alignment of interests can be explored by, among other things, examining the compensation scheme for the fund manager. Long-term thinking requires the formulation of a strategic process, and independent thinking is associated with self-confidence and self-esteem. Finally, many of these characteristics can be related to a person's entrepreneurial drive, which can be measured by using questionnaires.

Summary of Research Evidence Supporting the Value of Qualitative Characteristics

Researchers have extensively explored the value of intelligence in financial success and have concluded that high IQs and superior scores on aptitude tests are positively correlated with financial success and superior investment performance. Research studies exploring the value of education on performance, however, have yielded mixed results.

An investment manager's level of focus or work ethic may be hard to quantify, but academic research on the positive effects of entrepreneurial motivation on business success indicates that organizations with highly motivated

---

[27]See McCurdy (2012) and Towers Watson (2011).

managers tend to generate superior growth and profits. Scientific research on the importance of long-term thinking involved studying the effect of strategic planning on the financial performance of companies. Empirical evidence provides some support for the thesis that planners benefit from formal data analysis. This finding suggests that long-term thinking, if it does not introduce rigidity or discourage innovation, improves performance.

Alignment of interests has also been studied by evaluating incentive-based fee structures, the extent to which managers invest in their own funds, and the makeup of fund oversight committees. These issues have been explored for both mutual fund and hedge fund managers. Evidence suggests that funds with higher levels of manager ownership or higher levels of performance sharing are associated with higher risk-adjusted performance. The structure of mutual fund boards as a means for measuring governance quality has also been examined, and the level of independence has been found to be inversely related to fee levels.

Finally, researchers have explored the influence of manager characteristics on company financial performance, including portfolio returns, stock recommendation performance, and company profit margins. Both published and survey data have been studied for statistical relationships.

Although each study is unique, some basic conclusions are provided in **Exhibit 2.2**.

Exhibit 2.2. **Correlation between Manager Characteristics and Subsequent Performance Based on Investment Performance or Company Financial Performance**

	Factor	Relationship
1	Intelligence	Positive
2	Knowledge	Neutral to positive
3	Focus	Neutral
4	Long-term thinking	Positive
5	Independent thinking	Positive
6	Alignment of interests	Positive

The evidence supports screening for superior managers by intelligence, knowledge, independent thinking, and alignment of interests with clients. These criteria are especially important because most portfolio managers' compensation is determined subjectively instead of by using performance-based formulas.[28] Alignment of interests is associated with compensation, so it is useful to ask portfolio managers how their bonuses are calculated. There is no empirical evidence that links performance and level of focus.

---

[28]See Farnsworth and Taylor (2006).

Summary of Evidence for Retail and Institutional Investors' Manager Selection Records

Although the records of retail investors' decision making have been studied for years, researchers have only recently examined patterns of manager selection by institutional investors. One would expect sophisticated, experienced investors to hire and fire portfolio managers on the basis of rigorous, value-adding processes. Interestingly, institutional and retail investors alike seem to follow short-term performance trends and make value-destroying decisions when hiring and firing.

Research on mutual fund performance and asset flows indicates that retail investors focus on short-term periods, especially one-year and year-to-date periods of active return, and invest in funds that display strong recent performance. They also prefer low return volatility, seem to be influenced by advertising, and tend to retain poorly performing funds, possibly redirecting contributions to new funds but not selling out of old ones.

Conversely, institutional investors focus on active risk and strongly prefer managers who have outperformed in one-, three-, and five-year periods. They also appear to understand manager style, consider qualitative factors to a greater extent than retail investors, follow trends to a lesser degree, and behave more aggressively in firing poorly performing managers.

In terms of the performance of their investment decisions, both groups seem to destroy value with their allocations. Research on mutual fund investors indicates that their short-term (three-month) allocation changes yield short-term (over the subsequent three months) performance benefits, but their long-term investing patterns detract from long-term returns. Institutional investors lose money on their decisions to hire and fire managers over one- and three-year periods and do not appear to make up the losses, even after five years.

Indexing is a growing alternative to active management. Although it provides no opportunity to outperform the index and still requires the effective selection of appropriate benchmarks and portfolio managers, indexing provides assurance that the investment result will be close to that of the benchmark, typically at low cost.[29] Indexing also benefits from the reduced time needed to conduct new manager due diligence and monitor current managers. This investment approach is discussed in the next chapter.

---

[29]Managers could outperform the index if they pursue "active" strategies, such as early purchase of new index constituents.

3. Index Fund Investing

Costs and Benefits of Index Fund Investing

The goal of investing in index funds (indexing) is to replicate the performance of a prespecified equity or fixed-income benchmark. An index manager provides an investor with inexpensive access to returns on the market, or low-cost beta exposure. The term "passive management" is sometimes used to describe indexing, but it does not truly reflect the skill that index fund managers need to have to deliver accurate results, which in many cases are defined by deviations of a single basis point relative to the published index. Passive management more accurately reflects the decision of the investor not to pursue the challenge of seeking investment manager alpha. An investor can decide that the variability and uncertainty of returns and alphas does not justify paying active-size fees, at least for some mandates. The term passive also inaccurately describes indexing because the index investor outsources many active decisions, particularly to the management of the companies that constitute the index.[30] Managements at the companies underlying the index actively pursue business and financing decisions all the time.

The goal of an index fund manager is to track a prespecified index as closely as possible. The measure for replication success is called "tracking error" (sometimes called "tracking risk" or "tracking tolerance"), and the acceptable level depends on both the relevant security market and the size, liquidity, and stability of the index. Index construction and maintenance rules also affect the ability of an index manager to succeed (or even outperform). In technical terms, the manager's goal is to build a portfolio with a beta of 1.00, an alpha of 0.00, and an error term variance equal to 0.00, as illustrated by the following: If $\beta = 1.00$, $\alpha = 0.00$, and $\text{Variance}(e_t) = 0.00$, then

$$R_{P,t} = R_{M,t} \qquad (4)$$

in all periods t.

As a reference for common values of alpha, beta, and tracking risk, **Table 3.1** lists performance statistics for four equity index mutual funds and one bond index mutual fund. Alphas gross of expense ratios are, in most cases, close to zero. Betas are close to one in two of five cases. The standard deviations of the error terms range from 0.08% for the large-cap S&P 500 Index fund to 1.21% for the equity index fund tracking the MSCI Pacific Basin Index. The US equity markets are highly liquid, and the S&P 500 fund has

---

[30]See Grossman (1995).

©2013 The Research Foundation of CFA Institute

Table 3.1. Index Fund Alphas, Betas, and Tracking Error Standard Deviations, 1993–2011

Style	Benchmark	Alpha	Beta	Standard Deviation of Error
Large-cap US equity	S&P 500	0.08%	0.994	0.08%
Small-cap US equity	Russell 2000/MSCI 1750	0.71	1.003	0.75
Investment-grade US fixed	Barclays Total Bond	0.02	0.961	0.46
Pacific basin equity[a]	MSCI Pacific Basin Index	0.03	0.968	1.21
European equity[a]	MSCI Europe Index	0.03	0.963	1.64

[a]Data are from 2002 to 2011.
Note: The estimates are annualized and based on single-factor regressions using gross monthly returns.
Source: Based on information from Vanguard Funds.

an easy-to-trade futures contract available that matches the underlying index. The other benchmarks do not have similar advantages.

All funds experience daily cash flows that are commonly invested using derivatives. The small-cap index fund experienced a change in benchmarks during the observation period that affected the fund's performance.[31]

Fees for indexing tend to be lower than those charged for active management. They also tend to be lower for portfolios with larger amounts of assets under management and more liquid underlying securities and for portfolios that track indices with readily available futures contracts. For example, S&P 500 mutual fund management fees range from 6 bps to 135 bps,[32] with a mean of 18 bps.[33] **Table 3.2** shows fee levels for all mutual funds and index mutual funds in 18 countries versus a broad universe of benchmarks. The data are based on estimates from using several regression models to control for domicile, investment objective, and other characteristics. In this analysis, index fund management fees are 40%–67% lower than fees for the average mutual fund, depending on the model. The

---

[31]Later in this chapter, I note that some indices, particularly the Russell 2000 Index, have experienced run-ups in the prices of stocks that will soon enter the index. Index managers can profit by buying before their competitors. Some hedge fund managers, cognizant of the index reconstitution rules, may also buy up stocks expected to be added to the index for resale to index fund managers at higher prices. In the case of the Russell 2000, the index provider tried to remedy this situation by changing the frequency of reconstitution from annual to continuous. Since this change, the mean alpha of the Russell 2000 Index fund is 30 bps and the standard deviation is 10 bps.

[32]Clearly, something is odd when an index mutual fund charges 1.35% a year; it may be tied to an insurance benefit.

[33]See Elton, Gruber, and Busse (2004).

Table 3.2.   Annual Management Fees for Index and Active Mutual Funds in 18 Countries

	Management Fees	Total Expense Ratio	Cost Ratio Including Loads
All funds			
Mean	0.74%	1.05%	1.49%
All index funds			
High mean estimate	0.38%	0.43%	0.75%
Low mean estimate	0.17	0.35	0.60

Note: Fees are estimated using multivariate regression and are presented as a percentage of assets, annualized.
Source: Khorana, Servaes, and Tufano (2009).

analysis also indicates that larger funds and larger fund complexes charge lower fees.

Although accurate tracking requires skillful portfolio construction, efficient trading, and close attention to detail, the amount of resources required to manage index money tends to be significantly lower than that needed for successful active management. Lower costs allow for lower management fees. Indexed portfolio management is also heavily supported by computer tools, does not require a team of expensive research analysts, and typically involves less frequent trading than does active management.

Sources of Tracking Error

Sources of tracking error include imperfect security weightings (for example, those attributable to delayed adjustment to constituent changes), cash buildup (when the portfolio is not 100% invested because of income, corporate actions, contributions, or withdrawals), transaction costs (trading to handle constituent changes and cash flows), sampling error, and model error (because statistical models for building index portfolios that do not own every index constituent do not provide perfect forecasts).

Also, index portfolio managers may be responsible for scores of individual portfolios, which requires them to be highly organized and to set priorities carefully. The timing of portfolio rebalancing, for example, should ideally be determined by active risk levels for separate investment accounts rather than according to the calendar (e.g., once a month). Funds with daily flows, such as mutual funds, must be closely monitored and use sophisticated forecasts of cash movements.

The portfolio strategy used in index management depends, in part, on the specific benchmark. Passive portfolios of liquid, large-cap, publicly traded equities with limited numbers of constituents (e.g., the S&P 500) are typically managed using the "full replication" approach. This technique involves purchasing each security in the exact same weight as the index. Constituents of most market indices are capitalization weighted,[34] allowing for automatic index matching as prices change; the manager has no need to trade to maintain market-cap weights in the fund until there are changes in the index list.[35] These types of portfolios, including those tracking the S&P 500, the FTSE 100 Index, or the German stock index (DAX), tend to exhibit tracking error levels in the single digits. The use and understanding of risk models is not required for managing these portfolios.

Tracking equity indices with many constituent companies, indices of illiquid securities, or fixed-income benchmarks (because bonds typically do not trade in small lots and many issues that are not current may not trade at all) requires a "sampling" technique because not all constituents can be purchased. Effective sampling techniques go beyond random selection and instead require the use of statistical models that measure risk exposures and help managers build portfolios that are forecast to exhibit low tracking. Equity risk models include beta, style, and industry factors. Bond models are designed to explain term structure and credit risk. A key challenge for all models is to forecast future volatility, which, of course, is done imperfectly. Successful portfolio managers need to fully understand the shortcomings of these models and, ideally, use several systems to avoid biases in portfolio construction. For example, if the distribution, not just the weighted mean, of a factor does not match the benchmark, nonlinear returns to that factor may result in unanticipated tracking error.[36]

Appropriate Benchmarks

The indexing decision, like many investment decisions, involves comparing a known cost with uncertain outcomes. Both the cost of indexing a large-cap market-cap-weighted index and its tracking risk are small. Small-cap, illiquid, and custom benchmarks are more expensive to manage and generate higher tracking risk. Even though the level of noise may be significant in an individual portfolio, in most cases, it will be relatively small for the total plan. Therefore, investors should not be overly concerned with closely tracking an arbitrary index.[37] It may make more sense to be flexible with

---

[34]Many are adjusted for float.

[35]There is a cost to waiting because arbitrageurs can anticipate the purchase of new constituents; see Chen, Noronha, and Singal (2006) and Footnote 13.

[36]Recall that the CAPM is linear, assuming that the single beta, a constant, captures all market risk.

[37]Paul Brakke, a veteran indexer, made this point.

the benchmark and tracking level to secure lower fees and perhaps lower transaction costs.

Questions to Ask Index Management Firms during the Due Diligence Process

Investors who are selecting index managers need to do more than evaluate fees. They also need to be confident that potential managers can effectively minimize risk. A thorough due diligence process should include questions regarding

- replication, random sampling, or optimized sampling techniques;
- experience with risk models (if being used) and verification of model forecasts;
- trading techniques and cost estimates;
- methods for dealing with constituent changes and frequency of rebalancing;
- the number of portfolios per manager;
- manager experience;
- portfolio monitoring tools; and
- detailed performance track records, including tracking error, beta over different cycles, and individual account results.

It is also important for investors to look at the distribution of tracking error, not just summary track records. Long-term numbers reflect mean active returns rather than short-term variability. Similarly, a performance composite that represents a universe of accounts dampens reported volatility and underestimates the active volatility experienced by a separate account.

Evidence of the Value of Performance Track Records for Index Managers

Index fund performance, net of fees, shows evidence of persistence. This result occurs because no alpha exists to compensate for high manager expenses and error-prone management leads to inconsistent performance.

Elton, Gruber, and Busse (2004) studied the persistence of performance in S&P 500 mutual funds. Performance in this case is defined as both cumulative return and short-term error volatility. Not surprisingly, their analysis, which is summarized in **Table 3.3**, indicates that high management fees are responsible for most net underperformance versus the index and that past underperformance provides an effective forecast of future underperformance.

Table 3.3. Persistence of Index Fund Active Performance for S&P 500 Mutual Funds, 1996–2001

A. Mean annualized percentage gross active returns[a]

Mean	0.034%
25th percentile	–0.077
75th percentile	0.119

B. Persistence tests: Forecast coefficients and R^2

	Coefficient	*t*-Statistic	R^2
Gross active returns			
Three years vs. subsequent three years	0.265	2.328	0.119
One year vs. subsequent one year	0.221	5.170	0.073
Gross beta-adjusted active returns			
Three years vs. subsequent three years	0.665	4.558	0.342
One year vs. subsequent one year	0.126	1.649	0.025

[a]Estimated using expense ratios.
Note: Calculations are based on regression estimates of the relationship between past and future active returns.
Source: Elton et al. (2004).

They also studied performance gross of fees, which similarly tends to persist from one period to the next.

The authors used regression and rank correlation analyses to establish a positive relationship between past outperformance and subsequent outperformance. Once fees were excluded, confidence in the relationship declined. For example, regression R^2 dropped from 84.5% to 11.9%. The relationship was also less significant over one-year periods as evidenced by reduced coefficients, *t*-statistics, and R^2's. As with active management, although historical returns provide some insight regarding manager skill, investors need to look beyond performance track records when selecting index managers.

A two-step nonparametric test was used to confirm the regression results presented in Table 3.3. Gross active performance in one period was sorted and compared with gross active performance in subsequent periods. The results are summarized in **Figure 3.1**. A downward-sloping line in the figure is consistent with evidence that supports the persistence of good or poor index fund performance. The lack of smoothness in the lines, consistent with the low R^2 values shown in Table 3.3, demonstrates that using past active returns to predict future active returns for index managers may help in manager selection, but it is not a guaranteed

Figure 3.1. Persistence of Index Fund Active Performance: Subsequent Gross Active Performance of Managers Sorted by Past Active Performance for S&P 500 Mutual Funds, 1996–2001

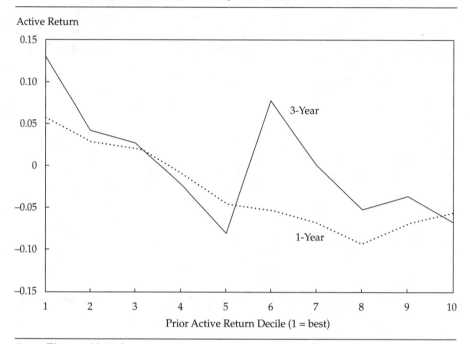

Active Return

Source: Elton et al.(2004).

technique. The results suggest that there is predictive power in identifying the managers in the top and bottom deciles, and in fact, the rank correlation statistic, even for one-year periods, is statistically significant. In other words, examining past performance can help assign managers to *groups* roughly defined by skill level, but it will not necessarily identify the most skillful one.

Index managers are paid to track the index closely, not to outperform it. Therefore, tracking results, in addition to cumulative active returns, is an important measure of success and may be a powerful forecasting tool. As with the relationship displayed in Figure 3.1, the relationship between past and future R^2 (measuring the explanatory power of index returns for fund returns) values can be determined by sorting the data, which is illustrated in **Figure 3.2**.

The lines in this figure show a positive relationship between past and subsequent R^2 values, but this relationship is not perfect.[38] Historical tracking risk may help identify groups of good and poor index managers but not

---

[38]In fact, the rank correlation statistics are not significant at the 5% level.

Figure 3.2. Persistence of Index Fund Benchmark Tracking and Subsequent R^2 Performance of Managers Sorted by R^2 for S&P 500 Mutual Funds, 1996–2001

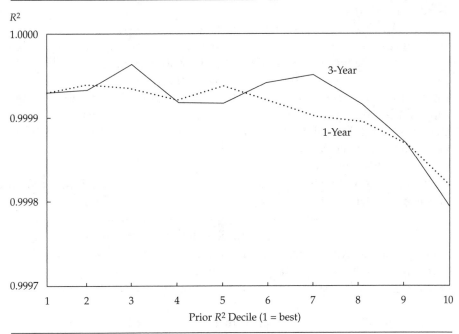

Note: R^2 is computed from regressions of fund and index returns using a single-factor model and describes the statistical power of index returns to explain fund returns. This is not a direct measure of tracking risk.
Source: Elton et al. (2004).

individual skillful managers. Both conducting further due diligence and hiring multiple managers may help reduce tracking risk.[39]

Additional Qualitative Information Supporting Index Manager Selection

Investors should seek index portfolio managers with good track records and well-run operations. A common refrain from pension consultants is that effective manager selection requires conducting (and paying for) a "qualitative" review of managers to supplement reviews of quantifiable performance. Consider this quote from the financial advisory arm of a large brokerage firm: "Our research is focused on a review of both qualitative and quantitative factors—factors that are designed to deliver a wealth of detailed information about the investment products available through our advisory

---

[39]Pooled index fund vehicles provide superior diversification to separate accounts but may be negatively affected by transaction (and tax) costs generated from inflows and outflows.

programs."[40] What better source is there for the important qualitative factors determining successful index management than the key skills valued by index firms seeking to hire experienced portfolio managers? These skills are listed in **Exhibit 3.1**.

Clearly, skilled index managers must possess a superior understanding of the techniques used to construct and maintain index portfolios, which includes knowledge of risk models and their shortcomings, the ability to effectively research and solve performance problems, and the talent to anticipate and address problems before they occur. Communication and team skills are also highly valued, and strong interpersonal skills help attract and retain clients. Indexing is a single-basis-point competition. Foresight and attention to detail may be the most important factors for producing close tracking.

Investors should pose several other queries to prospective index fund managers. What trading strategies do they use, and do those strategies add value? Does the firm lend out the portfolio's underlying securities, and how does it protect the investor from default? How are constituent changes handled? Research has documented what many index managers know from experience: Stocks being added to an index perform well in anticipation of the change, which creates opportunity costs for index investors who purchase these securities after a time lag.[41]

One study illustrated that prior to inclusion, stocks outperformed others by 3% and subsequently underperformed by that amount over the next two months.[42] As a result, seeking close tracking by purchasing new issues on their inclusion date rather than purchasing them earlier may lead to

---

Exhibit 3.1. List of Skills Required for Successful Index Management

- Extensive knowledge of index methodologies, portfolio construction, and risk management
- Experience with optimizers and risk models
- Strong research, quantitative, and analytical skills
- Ability to improve management processes
- Excellent written, verbal, and client communication skills
- Ability to work well in a team-oriented environment

Source: List generated from online job postings in June 2011 for index portfolio managers at large US mutual fund and ETF managers.

---

[40]This quote is from Morgan Stanley Smith Barney Consulting Group's information on manger research.
[41]See Chen et al. (2006).
[42]See Chen et al. (2006).

lower returns. In particular, close tracking can lead to a substantial impact on small-cap portfolios. Recall from Table 3.1 that the small-cap index fund experienced a tracking error standard deviation of 0.75%, compared with the S&P 500 fund's 0.08%. The small-cap fund also produced an alpha exceeding 71 bps, compared with the S&P 500 fund's 8 bps, presumably from the early purchase of new constituents.

Because mutual funds, commingled pools, and unit trusts are subject to cash flows, it is important for investors to have confidence in a manager's ability to invest them effectively. Does the manager maintain a cash balance for daily liquidity? Are transaction costs allocated to transition or current investors? Does the manager use futures contracts to gain exposure to the market? What is the process for anticipating cash flows if contribution and redemption information is available only after the market closes? Cash inflow patterns may coincide with rising markets and lead to a drag on performance if contributions are invested at the market's opening. Over a 10-year period, a 5% difference between cash and market returns would lead a 99% invested portfolio to underperform by over 75 bps. Data from Elton et al. (2004) indicated an average beta of 0.998 and a total 4.1 bp annual performance drag from uninvested cash, transaction costs, and other sources in the average S&P 500 mutual fund. Four of the five daily liquidity fund examples in Table 3.1 have betas lower than 1.00.

As shown in **Table 3.4**, a very small set of index managers dominates the institutional index management business, partly because of the business's economies of scale. Larger businesses provide investors with lower execution costs that result from internal and block trading. Experience gained from years of being in business helps guide portfolio managers at large firms to effectively handle index changes. Large asset sizes also allow for lower-percentage custody fees and potentially lower management fees. Broad systems capabilities and data sources, a global presence, and well-staffed trading desks help support high-quality operations for large managers.

Table 3.4. Largest Index Fund Managers, Ranked by Assets under Management

Ranking	AUM ($ billions)
1	$689
2	675
3	165
4	160
5	118
Next 45	539

Source: P&I (2006).

In-House vs. Outsource Decision

A few large investors, including corporate and public pension plans, manage their own passive allocations, but how hard is that to do? Full replication strategies are straightforward, requiring only pricing data, weighting information (capitalization and float adjustments), index constituent lists, and information on upcoming changes. A spreadsheet is all that is needed to compute necessary trades. If diligent, managing one's own S&P 500 fund is fairly straightforward. Stock lending can be implemented to generate fee revenue for large asset amounts held at a custodian bank.

But if the goal is to have absolutely minimal tracking error, then in-house managers must pay extremely close attention to detail. Income must be invested, execution costs must be controlled, and decisions on trading for constituent changes must be made effectively. Because professional index managers charge relatively low fees (in some cases, fees are zero after the shared revenue from stock lending is deducted), it is unclear whether managing index money in house is cost effective or prudent. This uncertainty is especially true if investors consider how outside managers provide clients with the upside of operational risk. Investors reap the rewards of positive errors and are compensated by managers for negative ones.[43]

What If Everyone Invested Passively?

Both securities analysts and market timers use current information to try to forecast future prices. This approach ensures that current security prices reflect, to some extent, current information and prospects. If done effectively, this process supports the efficient allocation of capital and improves the welfare of society.[44]

Market efficiency is dependent on the actions of active managers. The presence of inefficient prices motivates traders to bear the cost of obtaining information to profit from trading securities, which, in turn, moves security prices closer to their true values (reflecting all information) and makes markets more efficient. It is good news that earning positive alpha is difficult to do.

As Grossman (1995) noted, market-capitalization weighting in index funds must come from somewhere. An index fund is a sensible investment only when security weights make sense. French (2008) noted that "in aggregate, active investors almost certainly improve the accuracy of financial prices. This, in turn, improves society's allocation of resources" (p. 1538).

If all investors invested exclusively in index funds, security trading and price setting would be influenced solely by liquidity and financing needs rather than by information on underlying asset valuation and business

---

[43]This observation is from Paul Brakke (personal communication).
[44]See Hayek (1945).

prospects. Security values, both total and relative, would not accurately reflect fundamental opportunities for future cash flows, and as a result, the allocation of society's capital would be less optimal. The fact that investments may not respond positively to a growing economy or improved productivity negates the reason for investing in risky assets in the first place. Fama and Litterman (2012) noted that efficient markets require skilled active managers to compensate for unskilled managers. Efficient markets can be ensured, even with small amounts of actively managed assets, as long as active managers possess perfect information and trade at sufficiently high volumes.

4. Asset Allocation Policy and Its Implications for Manager Selection

Asset Allocation Process

The asset allocation process entails setting optimal weights of broad classes of securities, such as stocks and bonds, within a portfolio. Allocations are typically directed by one of two methods—strategic or tactical. A strategic allocation is a multiyear investment policy based on long-term investor needs and preferences, liabilities, and expected relationships of and between asset class returns. The allocation can be either fixed or designed to follow a predetermined path that is influenced by time, changing wealth levels, and varying investor preferences. A tactical allocation is a short-term policy that adjusts to changing expectations for the market. For example, investors who believe the stock market is overvalued may temporarily reduce their exposure to equities until confidence in earning attractive returns is restored. Some investors may adopt fixed strategic allocation policies and, in addition, hire active managers to make ongoing tactical decisions, either within separate portfolios or as overlays to existing portfolios.

How Asset Allocation Influences Manager Selection

A sample of asset classes is provided in **Exhibit 4.1**. The more complex a set of assets is, the more effort will be required for manager selection. For example, selecting a large-cap equity index fund is relatively straightforward, whereas private equity investing requires a thorough and lengthy process of due diligence of managers and partnerships.

Exhibit 4.1. Major Asset Classes

Public Markets	Illiquid Markets
Domestic equities	Private equity
Overseas equities	Venture capital
Commodity futures	Direct commodities
Real estate trusts	Direct real estate
Hedge funds	Timber
Domestic fixed income	Private debt financing
Overseas fixed income	

Asset Allocation: Broad vs. Narrow Asset Class Definitions

A strategic allocation that includes only publicly traded securities can be easily implemented using index funds. Equities, including real estate investment trusts (REITs), can be assigned to a single asset class measured by a market-capitalization index, such as the MSCI All Country World Index (ACWI). The ACWI includes a large cross section of stocks in both developed and emerging markets. Barclays offers a market-cap-weighted global aggregate bond index that incorporates investment-grade corporate, government, and asset-backed fixed-income issues that can be used as a single fixed-income benchmark. If market weights of underlying issues are acceptable and the investor does not seek access to private investments, the IPS can then be implemented with only two indexed managers: one global stock manager and one global bond manager. This approach represents a very straightforward manager selection process that requires only two searches. Regular rebalancing of the two-asset mix is facilitated by the relative liquidity of the two benchmarks. This approach also minimizes administrative costs and management fees (from both the low-cost indexing decision and the declining fee schedules that result from higher asset balances), but it does not provide opportunities for liability matching, full diversification, or enhanced return.

Investors who want to control weights of domestic versus non-domestic, large versus small, and high-risk versus low-risk securities must complete at least six manager searches and commit to comprehensive monitoring. Expanding the portfolio further requires additional searches—for example, for managers of high-yield bonds, micro-cap stocks, and asset-backed and securitized fixed-income issues. **Table 4.1** provides a sample of allocations to sub-asset classes

Table 4.1.   Sample Sub-Asset Class Allocations

Class	Plan Weight
US equity allocation: State of Arizona, 2011	
Large cap	28.0%
Mid cap	6.0
Small cap	6.0
Fixed-income allocation: State of Ohio, 2012	
Core fixed	13.3%
Internal credit	0.5
Emerging market	3.0
Floating rate	0.7
Securitized debt	1.0
High yield	5.0
Global high yield	1.5
Liquidity	2.0

for two US state pension plans. Arizona's strategic allocation plan necessitates a minimum of three searches for domestic equity managers, and Ohio's program requires eight or more searches for domestic bond managers.

Recent Trends in Alternative Investments

Many investors seek alternative investments for improved diversification and potentially high returns, although these investments complicate the implementation process. Investing in hedge funds and private equity has been done for many years and has become an increasingly important option following the 2000–02 bear market, during which many alternative investments outperformed the public equity markets. This trend is illustrated in **Table 4.2**, which shows the proportion of pension assets invested in "other" investments, including hedge funds, private equity, and real estate between 1995 and 2010.

As the table shows, investments in alternatives grew from 5% to 19% of pension assets. This trend necessitates a thorough understanding of these management techniques as well as additional resources for selecting and monitoring highly specialized managers. Alternative investing typically involves actively managed, concentrated portfolios that require the hiring of multiple managers to diversify portfolio risk. Recall Table 1.1, which shows that the number of private equity managers is many times greater than that required to fulfill other asset class allocations.

Table 4.2. Asset Allocation of Large Pension Plans in Seven Major Pension Countries, 1995–2010

Asset Class	1995	2000	2005	2010[a]
Equity	49%	60%	60%	47%
Fixed income	40	30	24	33
Cash	6	3	1	1
Other	5	7	15	19

[a]Estimated from 2009 data.
Source: Towers Watson (2012).

5. Setting Weights for Active and Index Managers

Reviewing the Manager Selection Process

The manager selection process involves identifying skillful managers, conducting due diligence on the most attractive ones, and determining the proportion of assets each manager should control. Investors set manager weights to meet strategic asset allocation goals, capture alpha potential of active managers, and access the tracking abilities of index managers.

Implementing Strategic Asset Allocation

Once an investor's asset allocation has been set, the next step is to hire and fund portfolio managers to establish the target allocations. Finding the optimal mix of portfolio managers is dependent on the investor's expectations for alpha and attitude toward active risk as well as the manager's risk exposures. Investors may seek optimal trade-offs between active return and active risk or, alternatively, maximize active return while holding active risk to an acceptable level.

This optimization problem can be expressed as a mathematical model. The model's complexity depends on several issues, including the number of market factors, correlations between factor returns and active returns, and correlations between managers' active returns. In practice, volatility, correlations, and means vary through time, which further complicates the problem.

A simplified model representing this problem, assuming a single-factor return with zero correlations between alpha, the market return, and the error term, is laid out in Appendix C. An investor can use this model to choose a group of managers and determine appropriate weights so that the portfolio's beta equals one, so that the weighting provides attractive exposure to alpha, or so that active risk is acceptable.

Utility of Manager Selection

Assuming an investor's utility function can be expressed in common quadratic form,[45] the problem of setting manager weights by defining the expected utility of active returns can be conveyed as follows:

$$E(U) = E(rs - rb) - \lambda \sigma^2 (rs - rb), \tag{5}$$

---

[45]A full discussion of investor utility of return, including Microsoft Excel applications, is provided in Stewart, Heisler, and Piros (2011).

where

$E(U)$ = expected investor utility

$E(rs - rb)$ = expected active return defined as strategic portfolio return rs minus benchmark return rb

λ = constant measure of active return risk aversion

$\sigma^2(rs - rb)$ = variance of the difference in returns

An optimal level of utility can be determined (objective function will be maximized) by selecting portfolio weights that result in the highest level of $E(U)$ while satisfying portfolio weight constraints (typically, non-negative weights that sum to one) as follows:

Subject to $\sum_j ws_j = 1.0,$

$ws_j \geq 0.0,$

where ws_j is the weight of each manager j within the strategic allocation. These expressions raise two questions that are explored in the following two points.

1. *Why active return instead of total return?* Expected utility can be described as including total return where both asset allocation and manager selection are determined simultaneously. In practice, however, institutional investors rarely choose managers and asset class weights concurrently. They typically select managers only after setting an asset allocation strategy. Recall from Chapter 1 how investors write an IPS to define their strategic allocation and then subsequently set guidelines for manager selection. This two-step approach may be the result of a lack of confidence regarding alpha forecasts over long horizons or the desire to simplify the solution by breaking down the problem into pieces that are easier to solve (although the solution will be less comprehensive). Institutional investors may be comfortable accepting market risk but do not want their strategic allocation efforts to be overwhelmed by the manager decision. Although strategic asset allocation is set for the long term on the basis of long-term views, manager selection, especially for active managers, is based on short-term views. Asset classes have existed for centuries, but a portfolio manager's career is relatively short and can end on short notice. Grinold and Kahn (2000) proposed that this two-step approach occurs because investors (principal asset owners) and managers (agents) have different preferences. Principals accept beta risk, whereas managers carry residual risk. Investors worry about total returns and returns relative to liabilities. Managers are concerned about their returns versus their benchmarks and peer groups. They do not want to take on market-like levels of risk without receiving the benefits of diversification across managers that investors who hire multiple managers enjoy. Deriving optimal solutions by using quadratic

functions can be difficult. Optimal weights for assets can vary substantially even when expected returns change only slightly. As a result, changes in expected manager alphas could lead to large changes in proposed asset allocations, creating a cumbersome solution that would be difficult to implement.

2. *Total portfolio or single asset class?* Benchmarks are strategic allocation targets that may be set across multiple asset classes or for single asset classes. The utility optimization approach is best used for setting manager weights for a single asset class or sub-asset class. Running an optimization to assess manager weights for these classes is consistent with standard theory if the benchmark is an efficient asset sitting on the efficient frontier according to consensus estimates. This approach may result in some loss in optimization efficiency because correlation of active returns across markets (for example, exposure to the business cycle of both equity and credit markets) is not considered. But as previously mentioned, optimal solutions using total risk models across asset classes may not be stable, and single-factor models are not ideal for multiple asset classes.

Equation 5 includes several variables, which are discussed briefly in the following points. They are explored in greater detail in Appendix C.

- *Risk aversion* is commonly defined as a constant incorporating the investor's change in marginal utility with a change in cumulative return. Investors prefer gains over losses and typically dislike losses more than they like gains. In Equation 5, a higher risk aversion parameter (λ) reflects a higher degree of risk aversion (dislike of risk). A higher λ will lead to a lower-risk portfolio (and as a result, lower expected active return) for given alpha assumptions.

- In a single-factor or *beta* world, active beta will influence both expected active returns and portfolio risk. Optimal solutions will favor betas close to 1.0; however, a formal constraint is required to guarantee this result, as long as the solution is feasible.

- In the objective function, *risk* is described as active return variance. Assuming normality, the probability of outperforming or underperforming by a given amount is a residual effect of optimizing the objective function, unless additional constraints are specified.

Risk can also be described in terms other than active return variance. For example, downside risk, or the probability of underperforming by a certain percentage, can be incorporated into the optimization model by limiting probability. A portfolio can be designed for which the probability of underperforming by 1% or more in a given 12-month period is no more than 10%.

Standard deviation or downside risk can also be a target in a modified optimization model. For example, a term to represent a risk budget can be incorporated by using active return standard deviation or downside probability in the model. It can be defined within a constraint, and expected active return can be the model's objective function. The expression is

$$\text{Maximize E } (rs\text{–}rb), \tag{6}$$

subject to

$$\sum_j ws_j = 1.0,$$

$$ws_j \geq 0.0,$$

$$\text{Risk level} \leq B,$$

where risk can be defined either as beta, active return standard deviation, the probability of active return falling below a target, or value at risk (VaR).

Another approach for selecting optimal manager weights makes use of mean-lower partial moments (LPMs).[46] LPM defines risk as the sum of squared differences below a target mean and can be computed by using an assumed probability distribution or a historical return series that does not require the specification of a return distribution. The optimal solution yields a portfolio with a low level of volatility below a given threshold, such as 0% or –1%.

Active managers can have management styles that are not well represented by published indices. In these cases, a "normal" portfolio can be constructed as a custom benchmark. Custom benchmarks do not line up with investors' benchmarks. The delta between investors' benchmarks and normal portfolios—so-called misfit risk—can be incorporated in the optimization model by modifying the utility function as in Equation 7 (alpha is assumed to be constant for this expression, but a more complex model can incorporate a varying alpha), where rn is the strategic portfolio incorporating normal benchmarks in place of manager portfolios.[47] Alpha must be listed separately because normal portfolios are indices.

$$\text{E}\left(U'\right) = \text{E}\left(rn - rb + \sum_j ws_j \alpha_j\right) - \lambda'\sigma^2\left(rn - rb\right). \tag{7}$$

A standard optimization tool, such as Solver in Microsoft Excel, can be used to maximize the objective function. The use of Solver is illustrated later in Appendix E. Investors must specify risk aversion parameters and provide expected active returns as well as active return variance/covariance matrices to solve the problem. Alpha and risk parameters can be computed by using historical returns. Care should be taken to avoid selecting unusually strong periods of performance or low correlations that will tend not to repeat. It is

---

[46]The formula for LPM is provided in Appendix C, and Stewart et al. (2011) provided a detailed summary and sample applications of the approach.

[47]See Waring, Whitney, Pirone, and Castille (2000).

advisable to practice running optimizations using different utility functions and parameter values to gain a feel for the influence of different assumptions on optimal portfolios.

Investors should carefully study historical returns and not simply rely on summary statistics of optimal portfolios. Much can be learned from computing the frequency of active returns within particular ranges: the size and length of periods of poor performance (the percent decline is commonly referred to as a drawdown), the timing and size of subsequent performance, and patterns of cyclicality. A case study illustrating this point is explored later in this chapter.

Each of these optimization techniques assumes that manager selection decisions occur within a single period. In other words, preferences, expected returns, and risks are all assumed to be constant. As a result, these techniques may not provide flawless guidance for managing allocations through time because key variables will undoubtedly change. Conversely, dynamic programming techniques, which are commonly used by researchers, can be used to set asset class allocations over time. Although not commonly applied in the manager selection process, they could provide new insight to investors.[48]

Attractive Types of Portfolios

Utility maximization, risk budget management, and probability distribution targeting are all useful techniques for exploring optimal manager weights. In general, an optimal mix will be achieved when portfolios that offer high alphas and the low combinations of alpha risk and risk attributable to factor mismatch are weighted most heavily. Assuming a single-factor model and defining alpha as a variable rather than a constant, expected return and risk can be defined as follows (equations are provided in Appendix C):

$E\ (rs{-}rb)$ = weighted average alpha plus weighted average difference in beta exposure times expected excess return;

$\sigma^2\ (rs{-}rb)$ = weighted average alpha risk plus weighted difference in beta exposure times market risk plus a weighted average residual risk.

Not surprisingly, investors prefer high-alpha managers over low-alpha managers with identical risk profiles. Investors can reduce risk by hiring more managers (via diversification) or by hiring managers with low alpha risk, active beta risk, and residual risk. To limit active risk, ideal total beta should equal one, but it would likely require sacrificing alpha. Therefore, managers with unit betas or combinations of managers with offsetting betas are attractive.

---

[48]For example, as an investment horizon draws closer, changes in risk and asset values may lead investors to favor managers with different risk profiles.

Case Study

To illustrate how these tools work in practice, four funds were chosen from which to build a strategic portfolio designed to outperform a small-cap US equity index with limited risk of underperformance. These funds are an index fund, a growth-style portfolio, a value-style fund, and a style-neutral core active portfolio. Performance statistics for the four funds and four mixes of them, calculated from 10 years of monthly returns, are provided in **Table 5.1**. The index fund displays the lowest active risk and the closest beta match

Table 5.1.   Performance Statistics for Monthly Net Returns of Individual Funds and Fund Combinations, September 2001–September 2011

	Individual Funds			
	Index	Value	Growth	Core
Descriptive statistics				
Beta	0.99	0.84	1.04	0.91
Annual active return	−0.33%	1.00%	−0.23%	1.13%
Annual active standard deviation	1.68	6.98	7.79	6.13
% Annual active < 0%	52.3	50.5	47.7	51.4

	Fund Combinations			
	Equal Weighted	Minimum Risk	Maximum Utility[a]	Maximum Utility[a] (beta = 1.0)
Descriptive statistics				
Beta	0.94	0.99	0.88	1.00
Annual active return	0.52%	−0.25%	1.17%	0.00%
Annual active standard deviation	3.69	1.63	5.12	3.36
% Annual active < 0%	50.5	51.4	50.5	45.9
Fund weights				
Index	25%	93%	0%	50%
Value	25	4	40	0
Growth	25	3	0	37
Core	25	0	60	13

[a]$\lambda = 2.0$.

Notes: Fund combinations are alternative mixes of funds created by using various optimization techniques. Data are based on an in-sample, small-cap US equity mandate with the S&P 600 SmallCap index as its benchmark and using four live portfolios.

Sources: Based on data from Capital IQ and Stewart (2013).

©2013 The Research Foundation of CFA Institute

relative to the index. The value fund displays the lowest beta, and the growth fund displays the highest beta. The index earned 5.8% a year in excess of 30-day T-bills for the period, so a high beta would benefit performance.

Various techniques were used to construct different types of fund mixes. Table 5.1 illustrates mixes created in the following ways:

* equal weighting the funds,

* setting weights to provide minimum active risk (defined as the standard deviation of $rs - rb$),

* setting weights to provide maximum expected utility $[E(rs - rb) - \lambda\sigma^2(rs - rb)]$, and

* setting weights to provide maximum utility with beta controlled to equal one.

Portfolios were created "in sample" by using a full series of historical returns. Although no return distributions were assumed, the return history was assumed to be known in advance. As a result, the goal of this exercise is simply to illustrate, not backtest, these techniques. See the directions in Appendix E to create an Excel spreadsheet to run the analysis.

The equal-weighted portfolio yields a standard deviation of active returns of 3.69%. This value is lower than the average fund's standard deviation (5.65%) as a result of diversification benefits. The average correlation between active fund returns is only 15.8%. Because of this correlation, and despite the value and growth funds' high active risk, the minimum-risk portfolio includes positions in these two funds and also delivers less active risk than the index fund itself.

The two maximum-utility portfolios offer optimal trade-offs between risk and return but differ in their beta exposures. The value of the risk aversion parameter, λ, affects the optimal portfolios: A higher value will penalize risk and lead to a lower–active return portfolio but will not necessarily lead to a unit-beta portfolio. Setting λ at 2.0 results in an unconstrained portfolio that is heavily weighted in the two funds with the highest active returns: value and core. But the optimal portfolio's beta is only 0.88, which means it is biased to underperform in up markets. Restricting the beta to equal 1.0 in the optimization process yields a unit-beta portfolio. Despite negative active returns, the optimization system replaces the value fund, which has higher returns, with the index and growth funds because they allow the beta to increase (to 1.0). The growth fund acts like a "completeness fund" by neutralizing the misfit of having non-unit beta even though the fund does not add to the return. As a result of eliminating the beta bias, the frequency of negative 12-month active returns occurring declines from 50.5% to 45.9%.

Many investors who use active managers have limited tolerance for risk, regardless of alpha. The maximum target value for active risk is called the "risk budget." Utility can be maximized subject to an active risk constraint (such as an active standard deviation not to exceed 3%) or a probability of active loss constraint (such as no more than a 10% probability of an active return below –5%). Investors can benefit from the diversification of active risk across all managers, not simply within a given asset class; thus, it makes sense in theory to implement a risk budget at the total portfolio level that includes all managers. Maximizing total portfolio utility with constraints to match strategic asset allocations and betas is a way to meet those objectives, but, as stated earlier in this chapter, it is difficult to do.

Standard quadratic optimizers, such as the one offered in Excel's Solver tool, can be used to manage active standard deviations by using historical time series or estimated probability distributions. But either an integer-style optimizer or the assumption of a particular probability distribution must be adopted to control downside protection. In practice, many distributions, including normal distributions, have smaller tails than are observed in the markets, so assuming a normal distribution for downside risk management can be problematic. Some practitioners suggest using rules of thumb to address this shortcoming—for example, by assuming the probability of a downside event to be two or three times the level indicated by the normal distribution.[49]

One of the key issues in building a portfolio of managers using mathematical techniques, whether it is with one asset class or across multiple asset classes, is the lack of stability in statistical relationships. Investors are wise to closely examine past periods of market stress, not simply average periods, for clues to potential strategy failure. The 2008–09 financial crisis followed a pattern set by many past crises: Correlations between risky assets increased in times of stress as investors sought relative safety. Correlations between active risks may increase because of factor and residual exposures. As an example, consider the portfolios detailed in Table 5.1. Although the correlations between active returns averaged 16% for the full period, the level of correlation increased substantially in 2008 and 2009 to 31%. This increase was attributable to more than the portfolios' market exposures. Residual return correlation also increased, from 15% to 24%.

Costs

The performance analysis of the portfolio mixes summarized in Table 5.1 includes returns net of management fees and other expenses allocated to the funds. Costs associated with searching for, implementing, and monitoring managers were not included in the optimization process. Institutional investors commonly hire pension consultants to help with manager selection, and high-net-worth individual investors often hire financial advisers. Pension consultants

---

[49]See Coleman (2011).

may charge one-time fees for a single or multiple mandate search. Depending on the mandate criteria, the search may be expensive. Search and other costs can be amortized over the term of the mandate, deducted from future returns, and added to a utility function by adding a separate term. Within the optimization, portfolios would have unique search, implementation, and monitoring costs, and the weighted average cost would be subtracted from expected return. Index funds, which are associated with lower costs, would be favored in the optimization. The inclusion of search and implementation costs in the optimization process influences the dynamics of manager selection. Investors are less inclined to change managers when searches create new costs.

Consider the financial adviser business model. Financial advisers typically include the cost of manager searches and monitoring in their percent-of-assets fees, which also cover data collection, reporting, and asset allocation monitoring. **Table 5.2** shows that total fees are not insignificant.

Table 5.2. Average Annual Financial Adviser Fees Based on Assets under Management, 2010

Asset Size ($ millions)	Fee (%)
1–2	1.17
2–3	1.07
3–4	0.98
4–5	0.93
>5	0.63

Source: PriceMetrix (2011).

Quarterly or annual reviews of managers generate ongoing costs. The use of active managers requires more monitoring on the part of the investor than would be required for index managers, partly because of the number of managers, increased complexity, and reduced transparency of actively managed funds. Many active managers, such as hedge fund managers, are uncomfortable sharing information regarding trades and holdings. Investors who require this information to estimate risk in their portfolios will need managers who are comfortable sharing it. It is important for investors to consider all types of costs when formulating investment plans.

6. The Dynamics of Manager Selection: Performance Analysis, Monitoring, and Fee Incentives

Introduction

Previous chapters have addressed issues surrounding manager selection and formulating and implementing an investment program. In most cases, a one-period world was assumed in which investor preferences, investors' views on risk and return, and manager alphas did not change. But we live in a world where things always change. An investor's horizon, market characteristics, and manager alphas will vary over time. Also, estimation periods are commonly so short that good or bad historical performance results may ultimately be attributable to luck.

Consider, for example, a private equity limited partnership that will terminate after 10 years of operation or a hedge fund with an expected 5-year span. Investors can rerun single manager selection optimizations with new parameters to determine ideal manager weights, but it would be preferable to consider the long-term horizon and think about how individual investment periods, such as a year or a market cycle, should tie together. This approach would provide the opportunity to plan for manager hiring and termination within a policy framework instead of on an *ad hoc* or a reactive basis. Ideally, an IPS should specify prompts, independent of performance, for conducting additional analysis of current managers.

Investment professionals should use several different tools to evaluate their managers through time. These include tools to estimate alphas, compute performance attribution, and evaluate fee structures, including performance-based schedules.

Beliefs Regarding Active Management

Investors' views change over time in part because of growth in their skill and understanding of the investment business.[50] The opportunity to create value changes as participants enter and exit the marketplace. Asset classes that offer the best opportunities for skilled managers to earn alpha do not remain static, nor do preferred managers within asset classes. Moreover, investors' views on manager alphas change on the basis of observing their managers, learning from other investors' experiences, and formal training.

---

[50]Investors need to avoid being biased by their own limited experience.

Most positive historical alphas are not statistically significant because of a relatively high degree of statistical noise, which makes it difficult for observers to prove or disprove that skill exists by means of statistical analysis. Statistical significance of past results does not guarantee future alpha will be positive, although there is some evidence of persistence of alpha.

Arbitrage opportunities disappear and market valuations vary through time, so it seems reasonable to expect that alphas will likewise change. The fact that many active returns appear to move in cycles implies that projecting past mean results into the future is not the best way to forecast alpha.

How much evidence do investors need before their optimal portfolios include actively managed funds? Even a limited belief that skill exists may be sufficient to justify hiring active managers. This argument was put forward by Baks et al. (2001), who noted that even though statistical methods cannot prove with high confidence that a given manager has skill, it may be optimal to invest something with that manager. If investors believe there is a chance that at least one skillful manager exists and they observe high historical returns or other evidence of future positive alpha for some managers, no matter how statistically weak the evidence, they should invest a portion of assets with promising active managers.[51] But if investors have no faith whatsoever in active management, they should avoid it.

Use of Performance Data

Many investors carefully analyze portfolio performance to improve their confidence in a manager's alpha. They may also want to improve their understanding of a manager's investment process or track risk-adjusted returns. Performance analysis is commonly used to isolate security selection and to verify specific sources of risk and return. "Slicing and dicing" performance data by period and sector helps to identify whether active returns are driven by a single bias or factor bet or, alternatively, by multiple diversifying bets that change through time.

Although empirical evidence indicates that alpha tends to be short lived, performance analysis helps investors understand whether managers will perform well or poorly in the future and whether the manager's return pattern is likely to complement other investments. Style, leverage, duration, and credit biases can be confirmed and tactical bets can be uncovered by using performance analysis techniques.

Investors also need to be skeptical of performance track records. For example, they should insist that managers be in compliance with reporting guidelines from CFA Institute and review individual portfolio returns in

---

[51]Research suggests that investors should first examine a portfolio manager's abilities and only subsequently study performance data for evidence of skill.

addition to composite returns. Investors should also beware of benchmarks that change over time. Unscrupulous managers can game the system by selecting worse-performing benchmarks after the fact.

Measuring Alpha through Time

Investors select managers to implement their strategic asset allocations. On the basis of their beliefs regarding opportunities for active management, they identify which asset classes and sub-asset classes they want to assign to active managers. The source of active returns, a manager's active exposures (both intended and residual), and variability are all driven by the manager's investment process, including portfolio construction techniques. It is useful to conduct an analysis of portfolio exposures and performance to thoroughly understand this process, to confirm that the strategy behaves as expected, and to uncover unexpected biases.

Studying current and past portfolio risk characteristics in addition to performance is a good way to conduct these analyses. Equity and fixed-income risk models incorporate numerous factors to assess. To review fixed-income managers, investors should look at duration, convexity, term structure exposures, distribution of security positions, credit exposure (both sector and quality), predicted beta, and active risk forecasts.[52] To review equity managers, they should examine cash positions, derivative positions, sector exposures, regional and country exposures, style characteristics, and beta and active risk measures. When performance suffers, it is important to know whether a portfolio's positioning is consistent with past experience. Even better, investors can monitor exposures in real time to anticipate potential problems.

Common performance attribution techniques include holdings-based attribution, fundamental-based systems, regression-based techniques utilizing broad indices, and regression-based techniques based on factor returns. These yield estimations should be confirmed by alternative methods. This chapter explains two easy-to-apply performance analysis techniques—holdings-based attribution and regression-based attribution using factor returns.

Holdings-Based Attribution

Holdings-based techniques, such as the Brinson approach, are popular for computing performance attribution because they do not rely on risk models or regression assumptions.[53] Brinson attribution, named for investment

---

[52]Risk forecasts can be estimated from historical data or forecasts, including using measures provided by vendors, such as BARRA, which may provide a breakdown of the sources of risk.
[53]The Brinson technique is especially popular for monthly or quarterly analyses. Compounding results across periods is cumbersome in Excel.

manager Gary Brinson, decomposes returns into the allocation effect (categories include asset class, style within asset class, and sector within style) and the selection effect (the residual return).[54] Active weights of categories are multiplied by benchmark category returns to determine the allocation effect. The difference between category returns (portfolio minus benchmark) times the benchmark category weight provides the selection return, as illustrated in the following equations based on a two-component model.

$$\text{Allocation} = \sum_i \left(ws_{Ci} - wb_{Ci} \right) rb_{Ci}. \tag{8}$$

$$\text{Selection} \;\; = \sum_i wb_{Ci} \left(rs_{Ci} - rb_{Ci} \right). \tag{9}$$

$$\text{Interaction} = \sum_i \left(ws_{Ci} - wb_{Ci} \right)\left(rs_{Ci} - rb_{Ci} \right), \tag{10}$$

where

ws_{Ci} = selected portfolio's weight in category i

wb_{Ci} = benchmark portfolio's weight in category i

rs_{Ci} = return of category i within the selected portfolio

rb_{Ci} = return of the category i within the benchmark portfolio

In addition, a portion of return, known as interaction or cross-product return, cannot be uniquely assigned (without further assumptions) to category or residual return. Attribution results can be compounded across single periods to evaluate the importance of changing exposures through time. Although the Brinson approach can be implemented using a spreadsheet without building a risk model, it assumes that betas within categories are 1.0. Therefore, it cannot address changing betas or leverage. Instead, it assigns the performance impact from betas greater than or less than 1.0 to the residual selection effect. The Brinson approach is commonly used in multicountry portfolios. A summary of performance attribution, with selection and interaction effects combined, is presented in **Table 6.1**.

Regression-Based Attribution

Techniques for estimating alpha (α) can be expressed by using the following, now familiar, equation:

$$R_{P,t} = \alpha_P + R_{f,t} + \sum_j \beta_{P,j} \left(F_{j,t} \right) + e_t, \tag{11}$$

where $\beta_{P,j}$ is the beta exposure to factor j and F_j is the return of factor j. Alpha is typically assumed to be constant. This expression represents the

---

[54]See Brinson and Fachler (1985).

Table 6.1. Sample Brinson-Style Performance Attribution Analysis of US Equity Portfolio: Sector Allocation vs. Security Selection and Interaction Effects

	Allocation Effect	Selection Plus Interaction	Total Effect
Consumer	0.24	2.95	3.19
Finance	−0.40	0.60	0.19
Health	−0.06	−0.63	−0.69
Industrial	0.15	−0.69	−0.54
Technology	−0.14	1.52	1.38
Cash	−0.31	0.06	−0.25
Unassigned	0.20	—	0.20
Total	−0.32	3.81	3.48

Source: Based on data from FactSet.

CAPM when $j = 1$ and F_j is the return on the market less the risk-free rate. Multifactor, fundamental equity models are constructed by estimating the return on factors (such as P/E) with the use of a cross-sectional regression across individual securities for a given period. This approach creates a time series of factor returns. The process is data intensive, and as a result, factor models are commonly provided by vendors.

Simple regression-based alpha estimation techniques use one or more market index returns and are commonly used to produce style analyses. These techniques are subject to statistical problems as a result of high positive correlations among index total returns. Another regression-based technique, the Fama–French (1993) method, estimates factor returns by computing the difference in returns between the top and bottom half of a universe of securities sorted by one specific characteristic (such as P/B and cap size for equities or duration and credit risk for bonds). This method also assumes that exposures to these characteristics remain constant over the observation period and that relationships are linear. The Fama–French method misses the sensitivity offered by professional financial software, which uses fundamental factor modeling and captures changing exposures over time, but it is useful for computing alpha for any given manager and is easily calculated in Excel, as illustrated in Appendix E. Given a data series, both single long-term alphas and multiple short-term alphas can be estimated by using this approach.

Table 6.2 presents alpha estimates calculated by using a four-factor equity model. A multifactor model provides more accurate estimates than a single-factor model.[55] The annualized alpha of 2.08% is derived from regressions for both the portfolio and its cap-size-matched benchmark. The Fama–French

---

[55]In this case, a single-factor regression model produces an alpha estimate of 4.94% (not shown in the chart) versus the S&P 500.

Table 6.2. Four-Factor Alpha Regression Estimates for Portfolio and Benchmark Performance vs. the S&P 500, 2001–2011

	Portfolio	Benchmark	Active
Percentage monthly alpha × 12	1.26	−0.81	2.08
Beta coefficient	0.90	0.93	−0.03
Size coefficient	0.74	0.79	−0.05
Value coefficient	0.08	0.25	−0.17
Momentum coefficient	0.07	0.03	0.04

Note: Data are based on monthly gross returns of a small-cap US equity portfolio and the S&P 600 SmallCap index as its benchmark.
Source: Stewart (2013).

multifactor approach can be improved by also running a regression on the *difference* in returns on the portfolio and its custom benchmark.[56]

Although the estimated alpha listed in Table 6.2 (in the Active column) appears attractive, at more than 2%, there is noise in the data such that the *t*-statistic is only 1.12, with a *p*-value of only 0.26. This result means that the analysis cannot confirm the presence of skill with a high level of confidence. Further analysis, such as studying peer-relative results,[57] would be required to improve confidence that the manager truly exhibited skill.

Risk-Adjusted Performance

In addition to performance attribution, investors want to understand the risks that managers are taking. Sharpe and Treynor ratios are commonly used to measure risk-adjusted performance but do not accurately gauge tail risk because they are based on the assumption of normal probability distributions. They also do not fully evaluate the risk of option-style payoff streams that are not symmetrical. Investors should examine such downside risk measures as value at risk and simple historical return frequencies and review market environments during periods of extreme active returns and alphas. One useful technique is to estimate betas and alphas separately in up and down markets. As discussed earlier, investors are wise to include risk targets in their management agreements.

Measuring consistency is another technique used to analyze performance that empirical evidence suggests is useful in the manager selection process. The frequency with which positive active returns are earned relative to benchmarks is an easy-to-compute measure of consistency that is related to traditional risk measurements. Performance attribution techniques can be applied

[56]A custom benchmark should help address some model misspecification. Javadekar (2012) shows that running a three-factor model on differenced returns allows direct computation of statistical significance of alpha.
[57]In this case, the results happen to exceed two peer group averages.

at the security level, and correlations between both active returns and alphas can be calculated to provide clues to a portfolio's construction process and subsequent portfolio return consistency.[58]

Management Fees

Investors seek strong performance net of fees. Managers charge fees to cover operating costs and earn a return on their capital—primarily human capital. A manager's fixed costs are relatively small and primarily cover the costs of technology and the long-term lease of office space. Variable costs, which are largely composed of payroll and marketing costs, dominate the income statements of asset management companies. Because a considerable portion of employee compensation comes in the form of bonuses, senior management can reduce bonus payouts as fee revenues decline to smooth a firm's profitability.

Investors are sensitive to management fees. In 2012, equal-weighted expense ratios for US-based equity mutual funds were twice as high as asset-weighted expense ratios, indicating that investors favor lower-priced funds and that larger funds charge lower expense ratios (ICI 2013). Recently, fees paid by mutual fund investors have trended downward. Expense ratios for mutual funds have been steadily declining over the past 15 years, after climbing for the prior 30 years. The asset-weighted average expense ratio was slightly higher than 50 bps in 1966 and rose to close to 100 bps in 1995 before declining to 77 bps at the end of 2012 (ICI 2013; Barber, Odean, and Zheng 2005). This change over time is partly attributable to the move toward low-fee index funds but also to an approximately 10 bp drop (on average since 1998) in expense ratios for both indexed and actively managed funds.

Investment firms charge fees in several different ways. Mutual funds charge fixed-percentage fees on individual investor balances.[59] Some classes of mutual funds, including those with reduced fees, require minimum balances. In contrast, institutional managers frequently offer declining-percentage fees on increasing account sizes for separate or commingled pool accounts. Institutional accounts frequently specify minimum account sizes or minimum dollar fees. Fixed-percentage fees facilitate managers' and investors' planning for future cash flows, whereas dollar fees are subject to the variability of asset values.

Fee structures can influence which managers will be willing to accept a mandate. They can also strongly affect manager behavior. Economic theory suggests that the principal–agent problem is complicated by the fact that an agent's skills and actions are not fully visible to the principal.

---

[58]See Stewart (1998).

[59]Although mutual funds may offer a declining management fee as fund assets increase, the individual investor does not (at least materially, unless the contribution represents a significant portion of the fund) benefit from investing more money unless the extra money qualifies the investor for a lower-fee fund class.

Although principals control the availability of assets, agents control both their expenditure of effort and portfolio risk. Moreover, the agent and principal may have different preferences—for example, each may care about different time horizons—and agents may not experience losses the same way that principals do.[60] Finally, total performance is to some extent beyond the control of either party. As a result of these factors, the principal's and agent's interests may not be fully aligned. In reality, managers are motivated to work hard even without incentive fees because they want to retain current clients and expand their client base and pricing power. But incentives are useful to help ensure that managers routinely act in the best interests of their clients.

Fixed Fees

"Fixed" (*ad valorem*, percentage of assets under management) fees reward managers who attract and retain assets, add value, and benefit from rising markets. Managers primarily grow their assets through skillful investing, hard work, and effective marketing. A manager's success in business, however, is also partly due to luck, especially in the short term. Managers benefit from rising portfolio values that are not only attributable to the combination of alpha and beta decisions but also, at least for long-only managers, greatly affected by market cycles beyond the manager's control. A decline in *ad valorem* fees as assets grow helps reduce the fee impact of rising markets on investors but does not eliminate it.

Once a manager's assets are large, he or she may not want to risk losing them. Assets are typically "sticky," which means that once investors allocate their assets to a manager, the manager does not need to produce as high of a return to retain them as he or she did to attract them. Empirical evidence suggests that to some extent, the situation is similar for mutual fund assets. To motivate such managers to work harder or discourage them from closet indexing, instituting an incentive fee determined by future performance may be useful.

Performance-Based Fees

Performance-based fees are determined by portfolio returns and designed to reward managers with a share of return for their ability to create value. Performance can be calculated from either total or relative return, and the return shared can be a percentage of total performance or performance net of a base or fixed fee. Performance-based fees are structured in one of three basic ways:

---

[60]For a summary of theoretical research on investment compensation, see Stracca (2006).

1. A symmetrical structure in which the manager is fully exposed to both the downside and the upside: The computed fee equals the base fee plus sharing of performance.

2. A bonus structure in which the manager is not fully exposed to the downside but is fully exposed to the upside: The computed fee equals the higher of either (1) base fee or (2) the base fee plus sharing of positive performance.

3. A bonus structure in which the manager is not fully exposed to the downside or upside: The computed fee equals the higher of either (1) the base fee or (2) the base fee plus sharing of performance, to a limit.

Performance fees are frequently paid annually and may include maximum and high-water mark (or claw-back) features that protect investors from paying overly high fees in the short term or for current positive performance before past underperformance is recouped. Private equity, hedge fund, and real estate partnerships commonly earn performance fees on total returns and typically do not limit the amount of the performance fee. Hedge funds commonly include high-water mark features.

Consider the example of private equity partnerships for which base fees are commonly applied to committed (not just invested) capital. Performance fees are earned as profits are realized, and invested capital is returned to investors. A common provision that helps protect private equity limited partners (the investors) is a requirement that the limited partners receive their principal and share of profits before performance fees are distributed to the general partner (the manager).

Specific performance-based fee structures are designed by both clients and managers. A formula is set based on anticipated distribution of returns and the perceived attractiveness of the investment strategy. Managers who can command attractive terms—for example, real estate managers who are in high demand and have limited capacity—have the power to stipulate the highest base fees and profit sharing in their fee agreements. Fee schedules are typically designed by fund managers. They are included in marketing materials and articulated in partnership agreements. Large investors can influence the terms of fee schedules or negotiate side letters for special treatment.

A simple performance-based fee, as illustrated in **Table 6.3**, specifies a base fee below which the computed fee can never fall. In this case, the manager is protected against sharing for performance of less than 25 bps. To make the result symmetrical around the standard 50 bp fee, the manager does not share in active performance greater than 2.75%.

Table 6.3. Sample Performance-Based Fee Schedule Showing the Base Fee and Minimum and Maximum Sharing

A. Sample fee structure

Standard fee	0.50%
Base fee	0.25
Sharing[a]	20.00
Breakeven active return	1.50
Maximum annual fee	0.75

	Active Return				
	<0.25%	1.00%	1.5%	2.0%	>2.75%
B. Numerical examples for annual periods					
Billed fee	0.25%	0.40%	0.50%	0.60%	0.75%
Net active return	≤0.00	0.60	1.00	1.40	≥2.00

[a]Calculated on active returns greater than the base fee.

If investment outcomes are the result of a mix of skill and luck (i.e., a probability distribution around a positive mean alpha), then performance fees constitute risk sharing. Fee structures must be designed carefully to avoid favoring one party over the other. Performance-based fees work to align interests between managers and investors because both parties share in the results. It benefits investors to pay performance-based fees, rather than standard fees, when active returns are low. Managers may work harder to earn performance-based fees, thus inspiring the term "incentive-based fees." Empirical evidence indicates a positive correlation between the inclusion of performance-based fees and higher alphas (and lower fees) for mutual funds and higher risk-adjusted returns for hedge funds.[61] Asset managers may consider performance-based fees attractive because they provide an opportunity to enhance profits on the upside and ensure guaranteed, though perhaps minimal, streams of revenue when performance is poor.

Performance-based fees can also create issues for investors and managers. Investors must pay base fees even when managers underperform. Management firm revenues decline when cash is needed to invest in operations or retain talent. In fact, the failure rate for poor-performing and even zero-alpha managers may tend to be higher when performance-based fees, rather than standard fees, are used.[62]

Performance-based fee structures may also lead to misestimates of portfolio risk. They convert symmetrical gross active return distributions into asymmetrical net active return distributions, which reduces variability on the upside but not the downside. As a result, a single standard deviation

---

[61]See Elton, Gruber, and Blake (2003); Ackermann, McEnnaly, and Ravenscraft (1999).
[62]See Grinold and Rudd (1987).

calculated on a return series that incorporates active returns, greater and less than the base fee, can lead to the underestimation of downside risk.[63]

Investors and managers may have different incentives when using performance-based fees. For example, according to a utility maximization model, fully symmetrical fees, in which the manager is fully exposed to the downside, tend to yield closer alignment in risk and effort than bonus-style fees.[64] Understandably, symmetrical fee structures are not popular with managers because of their impact on bankruptcy risk.

Bonus-style fees are the close equivalent of a manager's call option on a share of active return, for which the base fee is the strike price. Consider **Figure 6.1**, which shows an option payoff pattern based on the fee parameters defined in Table 6.3. In this case, the option payoff is modified by a maximum fee feature. The graph illustrates three fee components: a 25 bp base fee, plus a long call option on active return with a strike price equal to the minimum (base) fee, minus another (less valuable) call option with a strike price equal to the maximum fee.

Managers must retain clients from year to year, avoid poor performance, and not violate management guidelines. But they also have an interest in increasing risk, which may be in conflict with these goals. Based on option pricing theory,[65]

Figure 6.1. Payoff Line of a Sample Performance-Based Fee Schedule

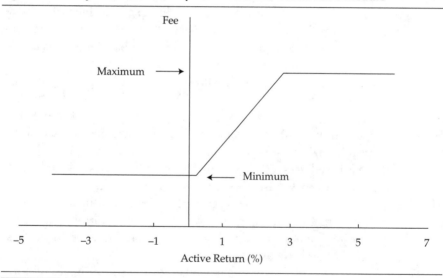

[63]See Kritzman (2012).
[64]See Starks (1987).
[65]Margrabe (1978) noted that an incentive fee (without a maximum) consists of a call option on the portfolio and a put on the benchmark. As a result, the value depends on the volatility of the portfolio and the benchmark and the correlation between the two—in other words, the active risk.

higher volatility leads to higher option value, which encourages managers to assume higher portfolio risk. This behavior is observed in the marketplace.[66] As a result, investors, when possible, should carefully select benchmarks for and monitor risk in their portfolios.[67] Senior management at investment firms should also ensure that their compensation systems penalize portfolio managers for assuming excessive risk as well as reward them for earning superior returns.[68]

Real Story: A Client's Free Option in a Performance-Fee Agreement

Consider the case of an equity manager in the early 1990s offering a performance-based fee that consisted of a 10 bp base fee and a 20% share of active returns in excess of the benchmark index (net of the 10 bps). The fee structure also included a maximum annual fee provision that reserved excess fees for subsequent years. Because there was no penalty for canceling the fee agreement, clients could opt out of the performance-based fee in exchange for a standard flat fee when performance was particularly strong. This option allowed them to avoid paying the manager's accrued, fully earned share and is precisely what many clients did in the mid-1990s, following a period of high active returns.

Other problems exist with performance-based fees. When managers have clients with varying fee structures, it is in their (short-term) interest to favor customers who have performance-based fees. Although this behavior is unethical and potentially illegal, managers can direct allocations for trades, deals, or IPOs to benefit the bottom line of performance-fee clients, to the detriment of others. It may be difficult for clients to monitor this activity. Fortunately, most managers act according to their clients' interests and recognize that such actions, once discovered, could destroy their careers or lead to criminal charges. Here again, due diligence, including the review of internal compliance systems, will help limit an investor's exposure to unscrupulous managers.

When managers can control the timing of the realization of profits, as in private equity partnerships, they have an incentive to hold on to property until it yields a profit. They may do so even when it would benefit the client to sell at a loss and invest proceeds outside the partnership. In contrast, hedge fund managers have an incentive to return assets in poorly performing partnerships when the high-water mark is substantially above current value (i.e.,

---

[66]See Elton et al. (2003).

[67]Starks (1987) noted that an investor can simply set a fee schedule that incorporates penalties for observed risk to align interests for risk levels.

[68]Although adding a layer of complexity to the evaluation process, an active-risk-adjusted bonus formula can be specified.

the performance-fee option is way out of the money). This choice results in the investor missing the opportunity to recoup previously paid fees with future strong performance.

Funds of funds (FoFs) commonly charge fees in addition to the fees charged by the underlying funds.[69] The fees pay for the investor's access to the underlying funds and for the FoF's due diligence, portfolio construction, and monitoring. In addition to these two sets of fees, investors are required to share the profits from well-performing underlying funds but incur the full loss from poorly performing ones.[70] To protect investors from paying overly high fees, hedge fund consortiums have begun to offer fee structures based on the total portfolio value of underlying funds, rather than on the sum of fees computed at the individual fund level.

Manager Selection through Time

Once there was a corporate pension plan officer who obsessively computed cumulative beta and alpha for his equity managers. "Beta of one and alpha of zero" he would announce month after month, but he never changed his strategy. The point of this story is that earning exceptional returns is so difficult that in most cases, when investors assume performance is average, they will usually be right.

Manager selection should be an ongoing process. Change should be guided by prompts and policies, not by *ad hoc* decisions or a reaction to changing objectives, benchmarks, or allocation goals. Despite uncertain manager alphas and imperfect selection ability, if investors can identify in advance managers who deliver added value net of fees, they can yield higher profits than if they invested in index funds. Investors who prove able to identify managers with positive alpha (for example, those who have a probability greater than 50%) earn superior performance over long-term horizons.[71]

It is very tempting for investors to fire managers who have recently underperformed and hire managers who have recently outperformed. Unfortunately, the primary benefit of this action is that investors no longer need to look at the fired, poorly performing manager's numbers on the next quarterly investment report. For most investors, this process leads to a destruction of value over time.

If it is assumed that active manager performance is cyclical, a common, though self-defeating, selection process can be described. **Figure 6.2** illustrates the hypothetical pattern of an investor selecting a manager after observing (or screening for) strong relative performance, typically over one-, three-, and five-year periods.

---

[69]During their heyday in the 2000s, it was common for them to charge a performance-based fee.

[70]Kritzman (2012) called this structure an "asymmetry penalty."

[71]Chapter 7 will review such a model, proposed by Foster and Warren (forthcoming).

　　　　　　　　©2013 The Research Foundation of CFA Institute

Figure 6.2. The Wrong Side of the Active Performance Cycle: Manager Selection and Active Performance

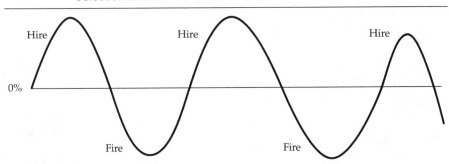

Ultimately, the cycle reverses and the investor suffers the consequences. Investors should be mindful of avoiding this type of decision-making behavior.

Unfortunately, empirical evidence validates this model. Ellis (2012) described a situation in which institutional investors are not aware that their process is flawed. Institutional investors' staff are not sufficiently experienced, consultants are quick to recommend the replacement of poorly performing managers, and investment committee meetings are not adequately productive. Chapter 7 describes the observation that institutional investors reallocate assets to managers with strong one-, three-, and five-year relative returns and redeem assets from managers with poor track records. Subsequent to these transactions, performance deteriorates. In two separate studies involving several asset classes, the performance of hired managers was inferior to that of fired managers following a change. Overall, the average performance of all managers retained by institutional investors exceeds that of newly hired managers. Studies suggest that the value-weighted average US equity portfolio held by institutional investors generates slightly positive (although statistically insignificant) net alphas, an improvement over retail investors.

Real Story: Periods Observed May Bias Investors' Views on Managers

Consider the example, illustrated in **Figure 6.3**, of an institutional investor that hires a small-cap equity manager with a three-year track record of 600 bps of active return per year. Results over the subsequent three-year period are mixed, so the investor loses confidence, terminates the manager, and invests the proceeds in an index fund.

Coincidentally, the investor's overseas affiliate, on the prior recommendation of the investor, still retains the same manager at the end of Year 2. After experiencing only one weak year, the overseas investor remains confident, continues with the manager, and enjoys strong performance

Figure 6.3. Sample Pattern of Active Performance and Hiring and Firing

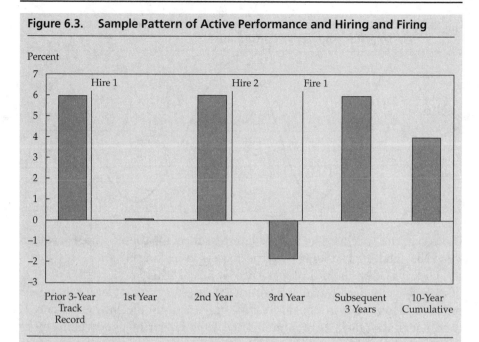

over the long term. This choice, in turn, leads to growing confidence, subsequent mandates, and additional funding from other affiliates.

The domestic investor, years hence, capitulates and rehires the manager. If the investor had stayed with the manager rather than reacting to mixed short-term results (the same results observed but not experienced by the overseas affiliate), the investor would have earned an extra 4% annually!

Track records for institutional manager selection should improve when formal processes are followed. A consistent policy should be followed over time to hire, monitor, and terminate managers. The policy should ideally fit neatly into the overall goals of the plan's investment objective, such as meeting a target liability within risk guidelines. Ellis (2012) recommended that investors spend their valuable time on the fundamentals of best practices and ensure that their manager selection procedures are well defined.

7. Research Findings on Manager Selection

Introduction

If some managers have skill, as evidence suggests, the next step is to identify them. That raises some questions: What ways are used to identify them? What traits characterize these managers? And can investors be successful at selecting active managers?

An extensive body of research reported in finance literature explores whether active managers demonstrate evidence of positive alpha, whether alpha persists once found, and the records earned by investors who hire investment managers. This chapter draws on general finance literature and business research on entrepreneurs who share traits with portfolio managers.

Part One reviews scientific research that explores both quantitative and qualitative techniques for selecting skillful investment managers. Qualitative factors studied include intelligence, knowledge, focus, independent thinking, hard work, and the alignment of interests between the manager and client. Quantitative factors include alpha measures, over both short- and long-term periods, as well as historical consistency measures of active return. Evidence suggests that skillful managers do exist and that their superior performance persists, at least before management fees. But in practice, it is not easy for investors to capture this added value, which is discussed in Part Two.

Part Two reviews the success of investors in selecting effective managers for both retail and institutional mandates. Almost all investors study performance history results before hiring managers. Institutional investors adjust track records for beta and style influences. Yet, both the average investor and the highly trained professional demonstrate mixed success, at best, for selecting managers who add value. In fact, most research results document a loss of value from these efforts.

Part One. Research Findings on Quantitative and Qualitative Techniques for Selecting Managers

Quantitative Measures for Manager Selection.
Research that explores the use of quantitative factors in manager selection focuses primarily on historical returns. This focus includes looking at averages, patterns, risk-adjusted computations, and alpha measures. Many studies identify

persistence by some measure of superior performance with statistically significant results, but the techniques used in those studies are not easily applied, in practice, to selecting individual superior managers. For example, the sample sizes in these studies are very large, so the techniques used would need to be applied to very large manager universes to be effective on their own.

As referenced in Chapter 2, US equity mutual fund alphas estimated over 36 months persist, with statistical confidence, in the subsequent year, although at a lower value. Table 2.9 summarizes how managers with top-decile four-factor alphas over three years generated, on average and gross of expenses, 1.9% alpha over the following year, based on research by Kosowski et al. (2006). Other studies have shown that alphas persist over shorter periods. For example, Blake and Timmermann (1998) found, using 23 years of UK equity mutual fund returns, that two-year top-quartile managers within four style categories outperformed both indices and peers in the subsequent month. Brown and Goetzmann (1995) found evidence of cyclicality in performance persistence from one year to the next in their study of US equity mutual fund returns from 1976 to 1988. They hypothesized that correlations between managers that are not explained by market-cap, interest rate, or equity style risk factors lead to this cyclicality. These studies suggest that using past performance can help forecast future winners, but not in all years; in fact, reversals of performance occur between some annual periods.

In addition to mutual funds, hedge funds have also been examined for persistence in performance. Jagannathan, Malakhov, and Novikov (2010) adjusted historical returns for style and option-like characteristics and discovered evidence of persistence in strong-performing funds but not in poorly performing ones.

Recent research on institutional managers has explored the persistence of active returns adjusted for factor risks. Busse et al. (2010) determined that for the period 1991–2008, US equity managers with superior one-year active performance continued their positive active performance in the following year but that this result was entirely attributable to a momentum factor.

One criticism of research on manager alpha studies is the use of ordinary least-squares (OLS) methods for estimating long-term alpha, which assume alpha and factor exposures are constant through time, potentially misestimating the presence of manager skill and persistence. Consider, for example, the data shown in Table 6.2. An estimation of portfolio beta based on 10 years of monthly returns yields a value of 0.90, but an estimation of betas over rolling three-year observation periods yields values between 0.75 and 1.15.

Mamaysky, Spiegel, and Zhang (2008) used a dynamic Kalman filter approach to determine whether mutual fund managers exhibit market-timing skill.[72] Using monthly data between 1970 and 2002, they estimated time-varying exposures to market factors to confirm the existence of dynamic strategies in the fund universe and to explore the persistence of market-timing alphas. Their approach included specifying alpha and portfolio beta parameters that vary through time.[73] The research techniques they used were an improvement over traditional OLS-based methods for identifying market-timing behavior and the persistence of timing alpha. This study also demonstrated a portfolio rebalancing strategy, using funds ranked by market-timing ability, that generated statistically significant investor profits.

Another study that did not rely on OLS techniques (Stewart 1998) showed that measuring the frequency of quarterly positive active returns can be useful in forecasting active returns and active return consistency. Stewart (1998) and Hernández and Stewart (2001) determined that creating quintile groups of institutional US equity managers by ranking historical frequencies of positive quarterly active returns was effective in identifying future superior managers over subsequent periods of three and five years. They found that ranking managers in the dataset by simple active returns yielded no predictive power. Hernández and Stewart applied these same techniques to global equity managers and found weak predictive power over three-year periods and strong predictive power over five-year periods. These results, computed for 1981–1996, are shown in **Table 7.1**.

Table 7.1. Five-Year Annualized Active Returns Following Rankings by Performance Consistency

Ending Quarter	US Equities	Global Equities
Q4:1988	1.43%	–2.24%
Q1:1991	1.55	4.33
Q4:1993	0.48	1.35
Q1:1996	1.87	3.45
Average	1.33%	1.72%

Notes: Active returns are calculated as the difference in annualized five-year returns on the most consistent quintile minus the least consistent quintile. Quintiles are formed based on previous five-year rankings of performance consistency, defined as the frequency of positive quarterly active returns.
Sources: Stewart (1998) and Hernández and Stewart (2001).

---

[72]They noted that standard OLS techniques lead to a high rate of false positives.
[73]They assumed that individual security betas were constant. Higher-turnover portfolios exhibited greater portfolio beta variability.

Qualitative Measures of Manager Attractiveness: Intelligence and Knowledge. Research that explores whether investment performance is correlated with measures of manager IQ or standardized test results has consistently found a statistically significant relationship. But the R^2 values are small in all such studies, which indicates that there are many factors beyond intelligence that determine investment success.

There is much evidence that documents the positive impact of education on income and wealth levels. But there is no overwhelming evidence that a manager's level of education is directly tied to investment performance. Empirical results from measurements of the value of advanced degrees and investment knowledge in determining investment success are mixed.

Zagorsky (2007) explored how intelligence, measured by IQ tests, and education, measured by highest level achieved, influenced income and wealth for more than 7,400 individuals. His results, for the period 1980–2004, indicate that education is positively linked to both income and wealth and intelligence is positively related to income but not wealth. Measurements of self-confidence, self-reliance, job consistency, and self-employment have a positive correlation with future financial success. He did not directly study indicators of risk tolerance or the ability to defer satisfaction.

Several studies have found statistically significant positive correlations between investment performance and the selectivity of a manager's undergraduate or graduate school. Studies have also found mixed evidence of a relationship between education and portfolio risk.

Gottesman and Morey (2006) tested the power of MBA program selection in determining the investment performance of managers who ran mutual funds in 2000–2003. They determined that excess performance is positively related to the average GMAT score reported by a manager's MBA school. With respect to the completion of advanced degrees, however, the authors suggested that there is no increase in added value from earning an MBA (unless it is from a school ranked in the top 30), the CFA designation, or a PhD. They also showed that the type of undergraduate degree earned (liberal arts versus other) does not have predictive value for explaining investment results. Busse et al. (2010) studied alphas of institutional equity managers between 1991 and 2008 and found positive cross-sectional correlations between manager alpha and the number of managers with a PhD employed by the manager's firm. They also found a negative correlation between alphas and the extent to which Wall Street research was used.

Chevalier and Ellison (1999) studied the mean SAT levels for managers' undergraduate schools relative to manager performance for 1988–1994. Portfolio managers who had graduated from prestigious schools tended to outperform peers who attended less prestigious schools on a risk-adjusted basis. This result suggests that managers from more prestigious schools may be brighter, may have received a better education, or may have developed more valuable job contacts (perhaps placing them in more highly skilled and resourced investment firms). The authors also concluded that there is no performance value, on a risk-adjusted basis, in an MBA, although managers with MBAs tend to take on more portfolio risk.

Kang, Li, and Su (2011) studied the influence that participation in the CFA Program had on the performance of sell-side equity analyst recommendations for the period 1994–2000. They found that investment performance, particularly for small-cap stocks, improved as analysts prepared for the CFA exams. Interestingly, risk taking (estimate inaccuracy and the difference between analyst and median earnings estimates)[74] declined and buy/sell balance (the number of buys versus the number of sells in analyst coverage) improved (more sells) for CFA Program participants.

The Value of Focus, Independent Thinking, Long-Term Thinking, and Hard Work. There is extensive research on the value of entrepreneurial drive, which is characterized by certain personality traits, an executive's level of commitment to a business venture, or specific skills that are commonly applied to ensure success. Research that explores the financial performance of small companies is not directly applicable to the selection of investment managers, but it may provide some insight. For example, executives who are tied directly to and passionate about their businesses and who can convert their energy into developing skills that address challenges tend to be the most successful. Goleman (1998) included the "love to learn" trait as characteristic of "passion" but also noted that the degree of a company's financial success is affected by the economic environment. These results are consistent with observations of experienced investment professionals regarding attractive characteristics of superior portfolio managers.

Baum and Locke (2004) studied the personal characteristics of founders of growing business ventures and examined small-company success over a six-year period. They provided a detailed review of prior research and observed that personality traits, by themselves, do not have much statistical power to explain success. For example, they noted that certain traits, and specifically the "need for achievement," have explained less than 10% of the variability of venture success. But they did discover that traits and skills (to some degree learned by necessity), both individually and jointly, offered strong predictive power for explaining company success. They also found that "goals, self-efficacy, and communicated vision," together with "passion, tenacity, and new resource skill," had a direct impact on venture growth and were interrelated (Baum and Locke 2004, p. 587). **Exhibit 7.1** illustrates these relationships.

---

[74]This risk taking could be considered career risk.

Exhibit 7.1. Characteristics of Executives and Their Influence on Venture Company Success

	Personality Traits	Executive Skills
Components		
	Passion	Ability to secure resources
	Tenacity	Ability to effectively communicate vision
		Level of self-confidence
		Tendency to set high goals
Influence on success		
	Directly	Directly
	Indirectly through skills	

Note: This list is based on statistical analyses of survey data composed of executives' characteristics and subsequent firm financial performance.
Source: Baum and Locke (2004).

Empirical studies have also explored the influence of industry factors, available financial resources, and the economic environment (growth versus stagnation) on company success. Wiklund and Shepherd (2005), for example, studied the financial performance of small firms to estimate the influence of entrepreneurial orientation combined with capital and environmental factors. They defined entrepreneurial orientation as a combination of being innovative, proactive, and a risk taker, which all relate to the culture of an aggressive investment management firm. Statistical results indicate that an increase in entrepreneurial orientation leads to an increase in a firm's financial performance and that entrepreneurial drive yields the greatest benefit in both resource-constrained environments and stagnant industries.

This result is consistent with the theory proposed by Stolze (1999) that experienced professionals with superior skills can apply those skills more broadly in small firms than they can in large, multilayered organizations. Interestingly, Zagorsky (2007) demonstrated that his study's measure of work effort (number of hours worked per week) is positively correlated with income but negatively correlated with net worth. Viñas and Stewart (2012) demonstrated that compensation was significantly higher for investment professionals who worked longer hours.

Results relating the value of experience to investment performance are mixed. Chevalier and Ellison (1999) concluded in their study of returns from 1988 to 1994 that mutual fund four-factor excess returns were marginally better for younger managers. They reported that this result could be attributable to younger managers' tendency to "work harder" in response to being at higher risk of being fired or to the fact that they have more years ahead of them than older managers do. Golec (1996), studying returns between 1988 and 1990, showed that manager age is negatively correlated with excess performance. His results also indicated that manager tenure is positively related to investment performance and negatively related to portfolio risk. Managers who build long careers as a result of strong performance amass higher levels of assets under management and may become more conservative to protect their records.[75] These results are consistent with those of Gottesman and Morey (2006), who showed lower portfolio betas for long-tenure managers and found that such managers exhibit lower turnover rates, which is consistent with relatively lower-risk styles of management.[76]

Investment performance can suffer when managers are distracted by sales or client service responsibilities and, as a result, spend less time on their portfolios. Large investment firms retain client service specialists who are knowledgeable of the investment process and effectively represent portfolio managers to protect their time. Smaller firms may lack this resource. Investors must decide how to balance their need for manager contact with the potential negative impact client service has on investment results.

The Value of Alignment of Interests. Investment managers and clients have the same goal: maximize the value of underlying assets. As assets grow in value, so does the wealth of the investor and the asset-based management fee paid to the manager. Strong performance also helps managers retain current clients and recruit new ones. But there are cases when a manager's short-term self-interest is not aligned with the interests of the client. These cases may include preferential treatment being provided to favored clients (e.g., the execution of a most-favored nation agreement), incentives being paid to client decision makers for the opportunity to do business (e.g., pay to play), or client assets being used to pay business expenses (e.g., soft dollars).

The risk of theft by investment managers has been recently highlighted by the Bernard Madoff, Allen Stanford, and Canary Capital scandals. To help limit this behavior, government and industry organizations, including the UK Financial Services Authority, the National Association of Securities Dealers, and CFA Institute, set rules and standards to promote ethical behavior from security traders and investment managers. But cultural differences influence standards of conduct, so what is considered appropriate by a given manager may be considered inappropriate by a prospective investor.

Scientific evidence supports the thesis that there is a benefit to investors when their interests and their managers' interests are well aligned. Multiple

---

[75]The study's sample does not include managers after they retire.

[76]Research has demonstrated that personal experience influences the amount of risk investors take. Market participants have observed that managers who experienced the bear markets of the 1970s or only the volatile markets of the 2000s tend to take on less risk than managers who grew up with the bull markets of the 1980s and 1990s.

studies illustrate that funds that feature performance-based fee structures, more robust governance structures, and co-investment by managers tend to deliver high performance and low fees. Portfolio managers' career trajectories are influenced by investment success, but in a majority of cases, manager bonus calculations are not highly dependent on investment results.

Management Fees. The business models of investment firms are based on fee revenues computed as a percentage of assets under management, expense structures dominated by staff salaries and technology costs, and levels of business growth driven by investment success.[77] As discussed in Chapter 6, fee levels relate both to the size of a strategy's expected active return and to its capacity. As a result, managers may seek to maximize assets under management in a low-capacity strategy with a strong track record (especially if the client needs to lock up his or her investment for a period of years) even when future performance is sacrificed. If managers value their long-term reputation, their self-interest will motivate behavior consistent with clients' goals. The incorporation of performance-based fees formally increases the incentive for managers to align their interests with those of their clients. Studies identify a strong correlation between the level of performance sharing and the level of risk-adjusted returns net of fees.

Ackermann, McEnnaly, and Ravenscraft (1999) reviewed hedge fund fee structures and tested for their influence on fund risk and return relative to mutual fund fee structures. Sharing was calculated as a percentage of total annual profit that was greater than a benchmark, and fee arrangements incorporated high-water mark features. As of December 1995, their database of 547 funds reflected an average performance sharing arrangement of 13.9% and a median of 20.0%. In the dataset, performance fees were most commonly offered in global-macro, event-driven, and market-neutral hedge funds and less frequently featured in non-US, bottom-up equity funds.

Ackermann et al. (1999) further explored risk-adjusted performance of hedge funds using a regression model to isolate the influence of performance fees on risk-adjusted returns. Specifically, they fit the equation

$$\text{Sharpe ratio} = f_i \text{ (management fee, incentive fee, US versus offshore, fund category)}$$

over the period 1988–1995 in two-, four-, six-, and eight-year intervals. They found that incentive fee sharing ratios were positively related to risk-adjusted returns. In fact, the incentive fee regression coefficient was the only consistently statistically significant value among all independent variables. The coefficient values are summarized in **Table 7.2**. The results indicate that funds

---

[77]See Stewart, Heisler, and Piros (2011) for a full discussion of the business model of an investment management firm and the incentives it motivates.

Table 7.2. Influence of Incentive Fee Levels on Risk-Adjusted Performance of Hedge Funds, 1988–1995

Test Period	Coefficient Value	Statistical Significance	No. of Funds
Two years	0.007	0.00	547
Four years	0.005	0.00	272
Six years	0.007	0.00	150
Eight years	0.011	0.00	79

Note: Coefficients are the result of a regression of the presence of incentive fees on the funds' Sharpe ratios.
Source: Ackermann et al. (1999).

with the typical sharing of 20% have a 66% higher Sharpe ratio than funds with no incentive fee. In a separate regression, they found that incentive fees were unrelated to fund volatility.

The influence of data problems, including the survivor, self-selection, and liquidation biases common in hedge fund data, was analyzed, and such problems were found to not influence these results. Another study, using mutual fund data between 1990 and 1999, confirmed the conclusions of Ackermann et al. (1999). Elton, Gruber, and Blake (2003) determined that the presence of performance-based fees was associated with higher alphas and lower overall fees—a double win for investors.

Governance. A study by Agarwal, Daniel, and Naik (2009) of hedge fund manager incentives described performance-based fees as a call option on the client's portfolio and confirmed the importance of incentives for investment performance. The authors further concluded that superior performance was also associated with "higher levels of managerial ownership, . . . the inclusion of high-watermark provisions," and "a higher degree of managerial discretion, proxied by longer lockup, notice, and redemption periods" (2009, p. 2221). Some of these features provide portfolio managers with the flexibility to maximize the values of their fund and, in turn, their fees. Of course, it may also be that skillful managers are more comfortable with incentive-based structures.

Higher expense ratios lead to lower after-fee performance, but interestingly, lower before-fee performance is associated with higher fees. An analysis of the impact of fees on mutual fund performance was conducted by Gil-Bazo and Ruiz-Verdú (2009), who studied the performance of US equity mutual funds. They observed a negative correlation between before-fee alphas and total fund costs (including annualized loads) and suggested that some management firms target investors who are insensitive to performance and then generate marketing expenses to attract them. By examining a measure of governance quality,[78]

---

[78]Morningstar's "board quality" grade includes factors on activity levels, independence, and work load.

the authors determined that higher levels of quality were associated with lower fees. A summary of all factor relationships is provided in **Exhibit 7.2**.

In their study of closed-end UK funds, Gemmill and Thomas (2006) found that higher fees lead to lower performance. They also found that fund ownership by managers and the structure of fund boards influence fund fees. Using data from 1995 to 1998 and controlling for fund size, age, and eight other factors, they determined that fees were greater for funds with larger boards and lower levels of board independence.[79] They also discovered that fees were lower for funds that had greater ownership by portfolio managers.[80] There was no statistical evidence that the extent of management entrenchment influenced fees.[81] Interestingly, Gemmill and Thomas found only limited evidence that governance factors influenced discounts for closed-end funds, which may suggest that investors are not fully aware of the value of good governance.

Another study that explored the influence of manager ownership on fund results was conducted by Evans (2008). She found that for the period 2001–2004, the level of investment by fund managers was positively related to risk-adjusted mutual fund returns and "inversely related to fund turnover" (p. 513).

Exhibit 7.2. The Influence of Factors, Including Governance, on Management Fees

Factors	Influence on Fund Costs
General	
Fund size	Negative
Fund age	Negative
Company size	Negative or zero
No. of company funds	Negative or zero
Fund turnover	Positive
Fund return volatility	Positive
Fund alpha	Negative
Investor fee sensitivity	Negative
Governance	
Governance quality	Negative

Note: Influence on costs was determined by regression estimates based on two studies on US equity mutual fund fees, characteristics, and performance during 1993–2005.
Source: Gil-Bazo and Ruiz Verdú (2009).

---

[79]Gemmill and Thomas (2006) defined board independence by "connections to funds 'outside' the fund-family" and "directors from the fund-management company on the fund board" (p. 736).
[80]Manager ownership was defined as shareholding by the fund management company.
[81]Entrenchment was defined as long notice periods for managers.

Portfolio Manager Compensation. Based on research results on incentives, investors should seek firms that tie bonus calculations directly to performance. Unfortunately, a majority of portfolio managers are not rewarded in this way. Farnsworth and Taylor (2006) reported that on average, 45% of portfolio manager compensation comes in the form of a bonus. The authors surveyed nearly 400 portfolio managers about their compensation structures and found that most bonus payouts were linked to the profitability of portfolio managers' firms rather than to individual investment results. About 37% (26%) of respondents said that index-relative performance (peer-relative performance) "had a lot of impact" on bonus computations, whereas 54% claimed bonus awards were "subjective and discretionary" (Farnsworth and Taylor 2006, p. 312). The authors also reported that only 25% of respondents stated that past performance had a large impact on salary. Large firms used objective methods to a greater extent than small firms, and very few portfolio managers (1.8%) were compensated on the basis of portfolio risk measures.

The Value of Long-Term Thinking. No formal research[82] is available in finance literature that explicitly examines the impact of portfolio managers' long-term thinking on investment performance. Swensen (2000) recommended that investors seek investment management organizations in which employee loyalty is well established to yield the benefits of long-term thinking. Academic research on long-term thinking has examined the effects of strategic planning. Miller and Cardinal (1994), for example, reviewed evidence from 26 studies and concluded that "strategic planning positively influences firm performance" (p. 1649). They noted that researchers believe the positive correlation results from executives conducting analyses, learning, and having better data. Research has also recognized potential downsides to long-term thinking; for example, long-range planning can discourage flexibility and creativity.

Part Two. Research on the Record of Manager Selection

Factors Retail Investors Tend to Value When Allocating Money among Managers. There is a belief that mutual funds and institutional products with the highest cumulative returns experience the highest level of asset growth, but growth is determined by more than trailing numbers. Products with the most consistent results over time seem to collect the greatest inflows of assets. And although one bad year may not be a problem for a manager, a year that is so bad that it affects long-term numbers will likely lead to outflows.

Research on the retail investing public has explored the relationship between mutual fund performance and fund flows. Retail investors tend to allocate money to mutual funds that have relatively strong short-term total

---

[82]At least that the author could find.

returns and positive short-term excess returns. They also focus on returns net of fees, do not like front-end loads, seem to be influenced by advertising, and behave differently in up and down markets.[83]

One example of this research is a study by Chevalier and Ellison (1997), which looked at mutual fund performance and asset flows between 1982 and 1992. The authors discovered that both one- and two-year trailing positive excess returns generated fund contributions and that recent performance had the greatest influence on the size of these flows. Year-to-date returns were also found to be relevant. Newer and smaller funds grew more rapidly than older and larger funds. To illustrate these results, a 10 percentage point outperformance (versus 0) in one year would lead to an 18.6% increase in asset flows in the second year and a 7.3% increase in the third year.

Retail investors tend to be less concerned with expense ratios than with performance net of fees. Also, they do not like front-end loads, they respond to advertising, and they are less concerned about poor performance for currently allocated money than about directing new money allocations. These observations were made by Barber et al. (2005) after examining mutual fund flow data for the period 1970–1999. Their estimated regression coefficients, provided in **Table 7.3**, illustrate how retail investors look to recent performance as a guide for allocating assets. The influence of past results on asset flows is substantial. For example, a 20 percentage point outperformance would lead to a 12% increase in assets, and a 20 percentage point underperformance would lead to a 4% decline. High costs, defined primarily by front-end loads, were viewed negatively. When advertising expenses (12B-1 fees in the United States) were isolated, regression

Table 7.3. Factors Determining Mutual Fund Asset Flows as a Percentage of Assets under Management in US Diversified Equity Funds, 1970–1999

	Coefficient	*t*-Statistic
Expenses	−0.389	−2.11
Prior-year excess return	0.393	11.89
Two-year prior excess return	0.166	10.40
Volatility	−0.596	−4.63
Assets	−0.009	−8.89
Age	−0.014	−8.76

Note: Data are from regressions.
Source: Barber et al. (2005).

[83]Shrider (2009) showed that absolute returns, compared with relative and risk-adjusted measures, are more important in bear markets for determining the level of redemptions.

results indicated a positive relationship between these fees and fund flows. This result suggests advertising dollars are well spent by portfolio managers.

Factors Institutional Investors Value When Allocating Money among Managers. Institutional investors are more experienced than retail investors, and an examination of their decision-making behavior suggests they are also more sophisticated. But they too weigh past performance heavily when allocating assets among managers. They tend to pay attention to consistency of trailing returns, recognize the importance of adjusting for style when analyzing performance, and incorporate higher hurdles in the selection process when hiring or firing managers than they do for simple changes in allocations. Institutional investors appear to consider active risk and use more qualitative information than retail investors do when selecting money managers. They also prefer funds with long track records.

Del Guercio and Tkac (2002) studied mutual fund and pension fund flows to compare the decision-making processes of retail and institutional investors. They found that active risk (the standard deviation of active returns) was significant in explaining flows in the pension fund sample but not in the mutual fund sample. The researchers' tests indicated that institutional investors relied more on qualitative information than did mutual fund investors. This conclusion was supported by the value of regression R^2's and by the fact that pension officers devote their workdays to studying investment managers. The researchers also found that institutional investors tended to be less influenced by trends than retail investors (lack of autocorrelation in pension flows compared with positive autocorrelation in mutual fund flows) and were more symmetrical in their decision making. In other words, institutional investors were more comfortable reducing current manager allocations than were retail investors.

Heisler, Knittel, Neumann, and Stewart (2007) examined fund flows and returns of active US equity portfolios invested for institutional clients, including pension plans, endowments, and foundations, using fixed effects regression analysis.[84] They examined the proportion of total flows to all investment products (defined as asset flow capture) received by a given fund in a given year, not simply flows as a percentage of portfolio assets.

Asset flow capture = f_A (cumulative returns, return patterns, and attributes).

They examined the importance of total returns, active returns, and patterns of returns between 1989 and 2000.

Heisler et al. (2007) observed that the sign (not level) of active returns over one-, three-, and five-year periods was the most important determinant

---

[84]Fixed effects control for potential serial correlation between observations that are associated with the same fund.

of asset flows. Funds earning positive active returns (relative to both the S&P 500 and style indices) in all three periods experienced the highest asset flow capture. Funds experiencing very poor one-year total returns experienced significant outflows. Total-account hiring and firing were associated with higher levels of active returns than were portion-of-account asset flows.

There was no apparent recognition of style "extremeness" or "beta" beyond style index assignments. For example, investors did not appreciate the difference between "deep value" and "relative value" equity managers. As with retail investors, institutional investors preferred small-asset-size investment products. But in contrast to retail investors, institutional investors preferred older products. Once a fund earned flow traction, it received subsequent inflows. In other words, when institutional investors and their consultants become comfortable or uncomfortable with a manager, their views persist. A summary of these results is provided in **Exhibit 7.3**.

Foster and Warren (forthcoming) developed a mathematical model of the manager selection process and explored several key factors that influence that

Exhibit 7.3. Summary of Tests for Determinants of Institutional Asset Flows

	Return Group vs. S&P 500	Return Group vs. Reported Style	Return Group vs. Beta-Adjusted Style
Total returns			
One year (sign)	Limited	Limited	Limited
Three and five years (level)	Limited	Limited	Limited
Active returns			
One year	Limited	Limited	Limited
Three year	Limited	Limited	Limited
Five year	Limited	Limited	Limited
Active return patterns			
One, three, and five years, all positive	**Positive**	Limited	Neutral
One, three, and five years, all negative	**Negative**	Limited	Neutral
Other patterns	Neutral	Neutral	Neutral
Attributes			
Young fund	**Negative**	**Negative**	**Negative**
Large assets	**Negative**	**Negative**	**Negative**
Past inflows	Limited	**Positive**	**Positive**

Notes: Limited is defined as some significant and some insignificant results. Neutral is defined as tests with no significance. Data were calculated as a percentage of total institutional flows using estimated regression coefficients of active US equity managers for 1989–2000.
Source: Heisler et al. (2007).

decision. Among these were the investor's skill at identifying positive alpha managers, the investor's investment horizon, and the tendency for the alphas of successful managers to decay as their assets increase. Investor skill was defined as the probability that an investor would select managers with positive alpha. Investors with selection skill were able to update their views and switch managers to their advantage to capture alpha net of fees, despite the assumption that managers, on average, generate only modest alpha on a gross basis. Skillful investors who were subject to high fees, such as retail investors, could justify selecting active managers when they had long investment horizons.

Institutional Investors' Views Regarding Factors Other Than Performance Records. Many pension plan sponsors and other institutional investors understand the challenges of selecting superior-performing managers. They scrutinize track records, adjust historical returns for manager style, analyze performance for consistency, and study manager risk. They also value a portfolio manager's ability to communicate with clients and the reputations of both managers and firms.

Payne and Wood (2002) reviewed the role of investment committees and explained that using committees, rather than individuals, to set investment policy provides enhanced opportunities for skill and information sharing and error checking. But making use of committees can also facilitate risk sharing and "loafing" (p. 100). The investment committees surveyed lacked diversity in age and gender, which could lead to biases in decision making. The researchers advised committees to be diligent in following guidelines and pursuing formal reviews of their processes.

Karim and Stewart (2004) reported results of a survey of more than 100 large US public and corporate pension plan sponsors regarding their decision-making processes. They investigated the hiring and firing of portfolio managers, the use of committee structures for making investment decisions, and the perceived effectiveness of the steps taken for manager selection. Consistent with the results of studies that have used asset flow data, in this qualitative study, 98% of respondents believed historical returns were important for manager selection and 85% required a three-year track record before considering a manager. Additional selection criteria included a manager's ability to communicate, his or her reputation, and input from pension consultants. Interestingly, committees that functioned effectively, those with well-educated members, and those supported by consultants tended to turn over their portfolios with the greatest frequency.

Foster and Warren (2013) conducted face-to-face interviews with Australian institutional investors and reported on the their decision-making processes, their views on choosing superior managers, and the importance of past performance in their manager selection decision. Overall, the decision processes were described as subjective, although they were supported by quantitative analyses to confirm manager claims, evaluate sources of performance, and determine a manager's ability to complement other managers. Investors claimed to prefer managers who could "articulate an underlying investment premise for that performance" (Foster and Warren 2013, p. 29).

The Track Record of Retail Investor Manager Selection. Research studies have reported mixed findings on the ability of individual mutual fund investors to select superior managers. Short-term (three-month) trends in mutual fund performance are common, and investors benefit from following them. But investors do not benefit from following long-period returns (one year and three years). Regarding index fund investment, retail investors in index mutual funds tend to select low-fee, close-tracking funds—but not always the best ones.

A report by DALBAR (2005) concluded that the tendency of mutual fund investors to chase (or flee) performance produces lower long-term returns than a dollar-cost-averaging strategy. In fact, the statistics provided in the report are quite staggering. They indicate that investors, on average, hold mutual funds for less than four years and consistently sell equity funds following periods of poor equity market performance, invest the proceeds in money market funds, and miss the cyclical rebound.

Academic studies suggest that retail investors profit from extrapolating short-term returns but profit little from making long-term manager selection decisions. Gruber (1996) studied flows between 1984 and 1995 for more than 200 mutual funds and found that investors earned positive post-flow alpha from funds reflecting quarterly money inflows and alpha savings by disinvesting from funds that experienced money outflows. Investors would have earned more than 14 bps a month for three months by swapping the two sets of funds, but the earnings declined to 6 bps a month for the subsequent nine months and 3 bps a month for the next two years. Frazzini and Lamont (2008) found that stocks held in mutual funds that experienced inflows tended to subsequently underperform stocks held in funds that experienced outflows over all time horizons greater than three months.

Zheng (1999) also studied retail mutual fund investors and determined that they exhibit a limited ability to select superior managers. She looked at investor weights and changes in weights in US equity mutual funds relative to returns between 1970 and 1993. Incorporating macroeconomic and style effects within a regression analysis, Zheng determined that asset flows were driven primarily by specific manager selection decisions, not economic factors. A summary of these results is shown in **Table 7.4**. Overall, the return on the asset-weighted average of funds underperformed the average fund (–5.8 bps per month versus –4.6 bps for the average fund). Mutual funds that received the largest cash inflows tended to subsequently outperform those that experienced outflows, but the funds with positive cash flows earned no excess return

Table 7.4. Performance of Retail Investor Manager Selection: Average Excess Returns Overall and Subsequent to Asset Flows, 1970–1993

	Monthly Excess Return (%)
Average fund	−0.046
Asset-weighted fund	−0.058
Cash flow–weighted (CFW) funds	
Positive-CFW funds	0.003
Negative-CFW funds	−0.103

Note: Excess returns were calculated as fund return minus the risk-free rate.
Source: Zheng (1999).

versus their benchmarks. Further study determined that the observed difference between the two groups was driven entirely by small-asset-size funds and that the return differences were short lived, disappearing within three months.

Elton et al. (2004) studied retail investors' abilities to select well-performing index fund managers. They explored index mutual fund flows and the performance earned in excess of that predicted by past performance and other characteristics for the period 1996–2001. Their goal was to identify whether investors perceived the value of low expense ratios and close historical tracking by managers in their selection process and whether investor decisions yielded subsequent performance benefits. The researchers discovered that retail investors allocated their cash flows more effectively than if they had simply equally weighted the available funds. But subsequent one-year returns were lower than both the fund-value-weighted average return (by 4 bps per year) and the returns earned by the top 10% of available funds ranked by prior-year performance (by 15 bps per year). Because better options exist, the authors concluded that there were other, unobservable benefits to using the slightly poorer performing funds (for example, the administrative ease of using a single mutual fund account) or that retail investors were not rational, perhaps swayed by the advertising efforts of the fund managers.

The Track Record of Institutional Manager Selection. Institutional investors tend to be more sophisticated than retail investors; they possess more experience and training, use more advanced techniques, and spend more time on the process. Research results indicate that the return for the average institutional manager is superior to mutual fund alternatives but that the impact on performance from institutional investors changing their manager allocations is negative.

Two studies (using the same database) looked at the performance of pension plan managers and found that US equity managers retained within the plans generated results superior to those generated in the mutual fund universe.[85] In fact, on average, the universe of retained managers generated slightly positive alpha (not significantly positive). This result supports the belief that even when the institutional manager selection process leads to a loss in value, the retention process, gross of fees, does not.

Several other studies looked specifically at the manager selection process. Goyal and Wahal (2008) explored the performance of 8,755 hired managers and 869 fired managers in the pension plan sponsor marketplace between 1994 and 2003. They found that on average, managers were hired subsequent to earning positive excess returns but earned zero excess returns after being hired. Fired managers exhibited the opposite pattern. **Table 7.5** illustrates that on average, hired managers underperformed fired managers

Table 7.5. Institutional Manager Selection, 1994–2003

	Cumulative Three-Year Excess Returns[a]	
	Pre-Transaction	Post-Transaction
A. Performance Based on Excess Returns before and after Managers Are Hired or Fired		
Hired	10.4%	1.9%
Fired	2.3	3.3
Difference	8.1%	−1.4%

	Percentage of Observations[b]
B. Reasons for Termination	
Performance	52.3
Changes at plan sponsor	
Reallocation to another investment style	19.5
Plan reorganization	6.3
Changes at manager	
Personnel manager	8.6
Regulatory action	9.3
Merger of firms	3.9

[a]Calculated as portfolio return minus benchmark return.
[b]Total excludes missing or not reported reasons.
Notes: Returns are for US and international equities and US bonds from 8,755 hire and 869 termination decisions. Data on reasons for termination are based on the sample of 869 observations.
Source: Goyal and Wahal (2008).

---

[85]See Bauer, Cremers, and Frehen (2010); Andonov, Bauer, and Cremers (2011).

by 1.4% over three subsequent years (before transaction costs). The researchers also explored the reasons for firing that were unrelated to performance, which was 44% of terminations, including changes at both the plan sponsor and investment manager levels. Interestingly, a separate test was conducted on a subsample of roundtrip transactions that indicated there was no impact on subsequent performance relative to whether a pension consultant was used or whether managers were swapped for performance or nonperformance reasons.

Stewart, Heisler, Knittel, and Neumann (2009) conducted a broad analysis of the manager selection record of institutional investors by examining the flow of assets within the universe of institutional money managers for the period 1985–2007. They also discovered that institutional investors did not add value by changing managers. Their review of more than 80,000 yearly observations confirmed that on average, institutional investors' changes in manager allocation led to underperformance in all asset classes. In fact, the authors estimated that the economic impact of manager selection changes, before transaction costs, was more than $170 billion.

The authors examined flows into the manager universe and between managers for each year, computed average manager returns weighted by their share of the flows, and conducted performance attribution analyses to determine whether the subsequent performance impact was attributable to asset class or manager selection decisions. The mean three-year manager selection subsequent return of -1.8% (annualized $-0.587\% \times 3$) is very close to Goyal and Wahal's (2008) -1.4% three-year figure. Cumulative return differences over one-, three-, and five-year periods for 10 investment product categories are listed in **Table 7.6**. Only 4 of the 30 values were not negative.

Karim and Stewart (2004) surveyed more than 100 pension plan sponsors and confirmed that institutional investors carefully evaluated past performance before selecting fund managers. The average sponsor believed that its manager selection process was appropriate and effective, which is inconsistent with research showing that institutional investors do not add value from manager selection. There was a subsample of respondents whose views were consistent with the empirical evidence. For example, those who had been unhappy with prior managers agreed that managers' active returns frequently reversed from positive to negative after they were hired.

An indicator of "performance chasing," based on the level of agreement with statements regarding active use of historical returns for selecting managers, was included in the study. This indicator was used to explore different levels of turnover and satisfaction with manager performance. Results weakly suggested that performance chasing leads to higher levels of manager turnover and performance disappointment.

Table 7.6. Institutional Manager Selection by Class/Style: Cumulative Return of Hired minus Fired Managers, 1985–2007

	Class/Style	One Year	Three Years	Five Years
United States	Growth	–1.5%	–5.3%	–6.2%
United States	GARP[a]	–0.5	–2.4	–3.8
United States	Balanced	–0.6	–2.1	–3.4
United States	Value	–0.7	–3.9	–2.1
United States	Core	–0.5	–1.1	–2.8
Global	Equity[b]	–1.3	–3.7	0.0
Non-US	Equity	–0.9	–5.1	–1.1
United States	Fixed	–0.3	–0.9	–1.5
Global	Fixed[b]	0.3	–2.2	1.3
Non-US	Fixed	0.3	–2.1	–1.6

[a]Growth at a reasonable price.
[b]Small asset size, beginning after 1985.
Note: Three- and five-year cumulative returns are reported annualized returns multiplied by three and five.
Source: Stewart et al. (2009).

A Common Manager Selection Mistake. Several studies have explored the importance of investment style for investment performance and shed light on the issue of manager selection. Teo and Woo (2004) studied the style behavior of US equity mutual fund returns and observed cyclicality. For example, a strong performance by value stocks was followed by a period of weak performance. This research documented empirically what many market participants believe. This research—combined with results by Goyal and Wahal (2008), Stewart et al. (2009), and Karim and Stewart (2004)—suggests that many investors are chasing the active performance of managers and buying late in the investment cycle only to experience a reversal in performance after the manager is hired.

8. Issues for Financial Advisers

Client Challenges

Individual investors, including high-net-worth and retirement investors, face more challenges than institutional investors in successful manager selection. They are subject to higher expenses and have less time to focus on investing. Individual investors are often less sophisticated and less experienced than institutional investors and, as a result, often seek the support of financial advisers. Financial advisers provide services similar to those of pension consultants but must provide some basic education to their clients in addition to investment recommendations.

Individual investors tend to be more focused on track records and less patient than institutional investors. When performance is poor, they become anxious, request changes in policy, or even terminate their relationships with their advisers. Individual investors are also less sensitive to benchmarks; they become disappointed with poor total returns despite superior relative performance. As a result, financial advisers need to manage their clients' expectations early in the relationship and continuously remind them of benchmark-relative targets and long-term objectives.

Smaller Balances, Higher Expenses

Individual investors typically invest in mutual funds. High-net-worth investors, however, may have sufficient assets to access vehicles offered by separate account managers. Minimums for institutional-style managers commonly begin at $5 million or more. In all instances, and especially for mutual funds, individual investors will pay higher—often much higher—fund expenses than institutional investors. Higher-percentage fees are the result of significantly lower balances. **Exhibit 8.1** summarizes differences between institutional and individual investors based on manager availability, accessibility, and expenses.

Some individual investors who gain access to institutional-style managers may need to pay additional fees to consolidators. As an example, fund-of-funds fees are typically calculated as a percentage of assets plus performance.[86] Because they pay a higher premium for active management, individual clients have a lower likelihood of earning positive net active returns. The burden of high costs makes selecting active managers more challenging for personal financial advisers than for pension consultants. As previously mentioned, under certain assumptions, higher investment costs lead to the longer horizons necessary for successful manager selection. A comparison of mutual fund fees and institutional management fees is presented in **Table 8.1**.

---

[86]See Brown, Goetzmann, and Liang (2003).

Exhibit 8.1. Availability to Institutional and Individual Investors of Investment Vehicles and Access to Portfolio Managers

Investor	Availability	Accessibility	Fees
Large institutional	Premium managers	Regular, portfolio managers	Lowest
Small institutional	Other institutional managers, funds of funds	Regular, portfolio managers and/or relationship staff	Lower
High net worth	Small managers, consolidators, mutual funds	Infrequent, relationship staff	Higher
Individual	Mutual funds, insurance products	Only published information	Highest

Table 8.1. Average Advisory Fees for Mutual Funds vs. Institutional Separate Accounts, 2005

	Large-Cap US Equity Fees (bps)	US Fixed-Income Fees (bps)	Average Account Size ($ thousands)
Mutual funds	70	48	27
Institutional separate accounts	53	30	41,049

Source: ICI (2006).

Table 8.2 lists average expense ratios, inclusive of advisory fees and other expenses, for US mutual funds. The lower value-weighted average indicates that investors tend to concentrate their assets in funds with lower expense ratios.

There are several forms of mutual fund fees, including sales commissions, loads, and expense ratios, and investors have different views about them. Over time, investors have become less tolerant of loads and commissions, and they increasingly prefer no-load mutual funds.[87] Since the mid-1990s, with the growth in index funds, expense ratios paid by mutual fund investors have declined on average and for both indexed and actively managed funds (ICI 2013). Funds with higher fees, including broker-sponsored funds, have delivered lower net performance (Bergstresser, Chalmers, and Tufano 2009).

Table 8.2. Average US Mutual Fund Expense Ratios, 2011

	Equity (bps)	Bond (bps)
Equal weighted	143	102
Value weighted	79	62
Active	93	66
Index	14	13

Source: ICI (2012).

---

[87]See Barber et al. (2005).

Other Issues

In addition to higher expense ratios, individual investors may face an additional cost that pension plans, endowments, and foundations do not face: taxes. Under most tax codes, individual investors must pay tax on interest, dividends, and realized capital gains. Profits earned from short positions in hedge funds are commonly taxed at high short-term rates. As a result, financial advisers must be well equipped to select tax-free bond managers and understand the benefits of tax-efficient equity portfolios.[88]

Finally, personal financial advisers do not enjoy the same access to top-tier managers that advisers to large institutional investors do. Also, because managers of separate accounts have high minimum balances, most individual investors must seek other, potentially less skillful managers. Individual investors and their financial advisers typically do not have direct access to their managers; instead, they rely on reports that their managers prepare. Individual investors and most financial advisers seldom have the opportunity to meet with managers, which limits the amount of objective information available for monitoring and can, in turn, lead to overweighting the importance of historical returns.

---

[88]See Stewart (1995).

9. Manager Selection for Global Markets and Alternative Asset Classes

Selection of Non-US Managers

Manager selection is a key issue for investing overseas as well as in the United States. Consider that US invested assets, although significant, represent a minority of global assets. For example, **Figure 9.1** illustrates that mutual funds, totaling close to $24 trillion in assets as of 2011, are very popular for investors in Europe, Asia Pacific, and the Americas excluding the United States.

Many pension plan sponsors actively invest outside their borders, as illustrated in **Table 9.1**, and this practice has increased over time. Between 1998 and 2012, overseas allocations by pension plans for six of the major markets listed in Table 9.1 have grown, on average, from 35% to 53% of equity investments and from 12% to 17% of bond investments (Towers Watson 2013).

US investors may expect overseas markets, particularly emerging markets, to be less efficient because of their less developed investment industries, lower levels of liquidity, home market biases, information asymmetries, and less publicly available information. But the arithmetic of active management also holds true for managers of non-US equities, as illustrated in **Table 9.2**.

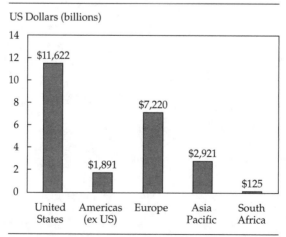

Figure 9.1. Total Managed Mutual Fund Assets in Various Regions, 2011

Source: ICI (2012).

Table 9.1. Percentage of Global Pension Total Assets Invested in Foreign Markets for Various Countries, 1998

Italy	0%	United States	11%
Singapore	0	Denmark	11
Malaysia	0	Canada	15
Finland	2	Switzerland	17
Chile	4	Australia	18
France	5	Japan	18
Germany	7	United Kingdom	18
Sweden	8	Netherlands	42

Source: Davis (2005).

Table 9.2. Single- and Four-Factor Alphas for US and Non-US Mutual Funds, 1990–2001

	Single-Factor Alpha	Four-Factor Alpha
US domestic	−0.85%	−1.21%
US international	0.14	−1.12
UK domestic	−1.02	−1.41
UK international	0.32	0.37
German international	−1.17	−1.40

Note: Alphas are annualized and based on OLS regression estimates for 4,384 conventional (excludes "ethical" mandated) funds.
Source: Bauer, Koedijk, and Otten (2005).

Fund managers, on average, deliver marginally higher alpha levels for international funds than for domestic funds, but the average alphas are not significantly greater than zero. Many individual non-US funds, however, do exhibit significantly positive alphas. Over 1990–1999, a large percentage of diversified international funds, including emerging market funds, generated significant single-factor alphas, but few regional or country funds did so.[89]

Alternative Investments

Alternative investments include hedge funds and investments in private equity, real estate holdings, and commodities. Manager selection for alternative investing is more complicated than for managers of traditional portfolios. For example, limited partnership vehicles are frequently used for alternative investing as a result of the illiquidity of their underlying assets and the

[89]See Tkac (2001).

commitment required by managers to implement specialized strategies over time. Limited partnerships that invest in private properties (companies, real estate, or collectibles) typically include commitments to contribute capital over a period of years (because attractive properties are not identified all at once). These partnerships often last up to 10 years, and capital is returned once the properties are sold. Many investors are willing to accept long time horizons and illiquidity in exchange for expected high returns from investing actively in infrequently traded markets. Characteristics of alternative and traditional investments are listed in **Exhibit 9.1**.

Investors in limited partnerships do not typically have an option to terminate their managers, so the manager selection process is more critical because the investor cannot quickly reverse a mistake. The selection process is also more challenging because timing is more difficult to implement. An investor may think that private equity valuations are low, but the process of identifying and funding a private equity manager could take years. Investment timing is mostly left up to the manager and the marketplace. Portfolios of alternatives are typically riskier than portfolios of publicly traded securities. They commonly include financial leverage (leading to high betas) and are concentrated, and in the case of venture capital, they rely on very large returns from one or two holdings for financial success.

Properties available for sale to private equity and real estate managers are limited at any point in time. Managers' access to the best deal flow, terms, and financing is key to their success. Private equity and real estate investments benefit from effective active management of underlying properties as well as attractive valuations. This situation puts new managers at a

Exhibit 9.1. Characteristics of Traditional and Alternative Investment Portfolios

	Publicly Traded Securities	Non-Publicly Traded Securities
Instruments	Equities, fixed income, commodity futures, REITs, high yield	Private equity, direct real estate, direct commodities, distressed
Portfolio construction	Diversified	Concentrated
Portfolio transparency	High	Low
Liquidity	High	Low
Funding	Quick implementation	Commitment implemented over time
Information sources	Much, publicly available	Much, privately collected
Fund accessibility	Commonly open	Commonly limited
Asset accessibility	Open	Limited
Asset ownership	Passive	Active
Leverage	Uncommon	Financial leverage common
Fees	Lower	Higher, performance based

distinct disadvantage, and scientific evidence substantiates that their invest-ment results are inferior. Performance records for alternative investment managers are summarized in **Exhibit 9.2**. These results confirm that inves-tors should look for well-established managers whenever possible, particu-larly for leveraged buyouts and venture capital investing.[90]

Lack of transparency is a problem for investors in limited partnerships. Many hedge fund managers do not allow investors to view portfolio posi-tions. Investors need to accept, largely on faith, that their assets are being managed in accordance with their expectations. Performance databases are frequently subject to survivor and self-reporting biases. As a result, investors need to be careful when assessing total industry performance.

Alternative portfolios commonly incorporate leverage, non-linear-payoff option-like exposures, and other unusual characteristics that make linear risk measurement problematic. As a result, return standard deviation is a poor measure of risk. Management fees charged by alternative investment man-agers are much higher than those charged by managers of liquid portfolios. Despite the challenges involved in selecting and investing with alternative managers, hedge funds, private equity, real estate, and commodities remain popular with investors, as illustrated in **Figure 9.2**.

Hedge funds commonly hold publicly traded equity and fixed-income securities, currencies, and derivatives, but despite this variety, their liquidity is

Exhibit 9.2. Evidence of Alternative Investment Alphas Based on Results from Four Research Studies

	US Equity Mutual Funds	Fund-of-Funds Hedge Funds	Venture Capital	Private Equity	Real Estate
Evidence of positive average net alpha	Zero	Marginal	Mixed	Mixed	Marginal
Evidence of superior managers	Limited	Yes	Yes	Yes	Limited
Evidence of alpha persistence	Limited	Yes	Yes	Yes	Limited
Evidence of flows to positive-alpha managers	Yes	Yes	Yes	Yes	Yes

Notes: "Marginal" means there is some evidence of positive alpha but net alpha is not statistically significant at a high confidence level. "Mixed" means some evidence suggests positive net alpha but other evidence suggests only marginal alpha. "Limited" means there is evidence for a subset of the universe but that it is not necessarily sufficient for supporting profitable trading strategies.
Sources: The hedge funds study is Fung, Hsieh, Naik, and Ramadorai (2008). The venture capital and private equity study is Kaplan and Schoar (2005). The real estate studies are Lin and Young (2004) and Bond and Mitchell (2010).

[90]The evidence suggests that if an investor cannot access top managers, he or she should not invest in private equity partnerships.

Figure 9.2.   Global Assets Invested with Traditional and Alternative Managers, 2010

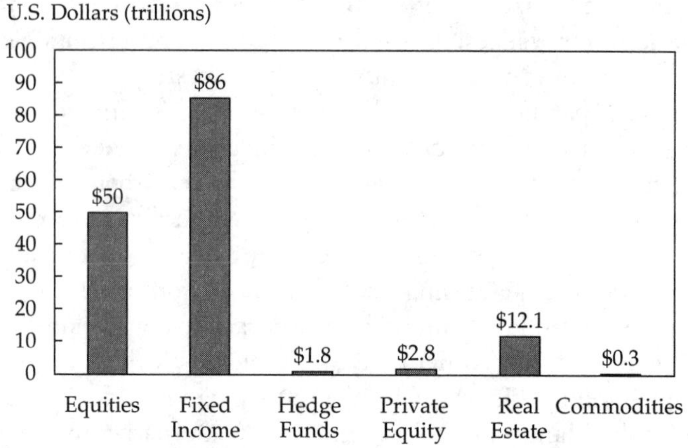

U.S. Dollars (trillions)

Sources: Based on data from Asset Allocation Advisor, Hedge Fund Research, Preqin, Prudential Real Estate Investors, and Barclays Capital.

frequently limited by redemption restrictions. Many funds of funds generate statistically positive alpha, but on average, they tend to produce zero alpha.[91] Their performance results are well aligned with the arithmetic of active management. Hedge fund alphas also seem to persist to some extent, and high-alpha managers (versus beta-driven managers) tend to experience asset growth over time.[92]

One concern associated with investing in alternatives is that some successful managers can earn sufficient revenue from management fees that they lose their incentive to earn performance-based fees.[93] Research evidence confirms that large hedge funds tend to produce lower returns than small hedge funds.

Some index portfolio management approaches allow investors to gain access to alternative asset classes. These include purchasing baskets of publicly traded private equity firms, real estate investment trusts, portfolios of commodity futures (replicating published indices; ETFs are also popular vehicles), and corporate bond index funds. Venture capital fund returns are hard to replicate passively, but they can be matched to some extent by investing in a leveraged NASDAQ index fund.[94] Investments in commodity trading

---

[91]Skillful managers should earn a higher portfolio alpha if they invest both long and short instead of long only.

[92]See Fung et al. (2008).

[93]As long as assets are sufficiently large, managers can make as much money from their base fees (and a zero active return) as they can from base and performance fees (and a positive active return).

[94]A single-factor beta of 1.66 versus the NASDAQ explains the return of a venture capital index with an R^2 of more than 60% (see Stewart et al. 2011).

pools, which commonly follow momentum strategies, can be (imperfectly) replicated by positions in derivatives.[95]

Alternative investments are subject to less regulatory oversight than standard investment vehicles, such as mutual funds, commingled pools, and separate accounts held at custodian banks. This oversight requires investors to increase their due diligence. Because alternative investments are typically illiquid, frequently include leverage, and are commonly opaque, it is critical that investors understand strategy risk and risk management procedures before committing capital. For example, investors should ensure that managers have systems in place to monitor risk, trading activity, collateral positions, and compliance.

---

[95]See Bhardwaj, Gorton, and Rouwenhorst (2008). As an example, SEI offers an index fund that actively trades commodity futures contracts.

10. Key Recommendations and Best Practices

Summary

This book is intended to help investors and managers alike understand the challenges of selecting superior investment managers. It also recommends best practices that are supported by theoretical and empirical research results. As explained, investors' goals and objectives influence manager selection, and as a result, the investment policy statement should incorporate a process for manager selection.

Several theories relevant to manager selection are reviewed. These include the arithmetic of active management, which illustrates that before costs, the average manager will earn average returns. A review of the efficient market hypothesis, the costs of implementing active management, and research evidence reveals that it is very difficult to earn positive net alpha. As a result, before implementing an asset allocation policy, investors must decide whether they believe superior managers exist and whether they can identify them in advance. As an alternative to active management, indexing can provide exposure to many but not all asset classes. Like active management, indexing incurs costs and its effective implementation requires diligence.

Asset allocation policy affects the manager selection process. For example, decisions regarding investing in public and private equities influence the level of resources required to conduct effective manager selection. Issues regarding setting manager weights are discussed in Chapter 5. The optimization of the expected utility of active returns is introduced as a technique to determine weights, and its application is illustrated with the use of historical data. This technique demonstrates that managers can be attractive because of their alpha potential and their diversifying characteristics. Performance measurement, performance attribution, and incentive fee structures are discussed in Chapter 6. Performance fees commonly improve the alignment of interests between investors and managers but can also lead to unintended incentives.

A large body of academic research on the issue of manager selection is reviewed in Chapter 7. Empirical results validate the arithmetic of active management, document records of poor manager hire and fire decisions for both retail and institutional investors, and demonstrate that trailing returns offer limited predictive power for selecting superior managers. More sophisticated techniques for manager selection, including

©2013 The Research Foundation of CFA Institute

measuring performance consistency and applying complex filters, offer promise. Research that documents the value of qualitative characteristics for forecasting manager alpha is also reviewed. The value of good governance, including incentive fee structures and joint investment, has been confirmed through empirical tests.

Issues for financial advising, investing globally, and investing in alternative assets are reviewed in Chapters 8 and 9. Financial advisers must deal with unsophisticated clients, high manager fees, and low manager accessibility. Empirical evidence indicates that the arithmetic of active management also applies in global markets. Investing in alternative assets requires extensive due diligence to make up for extended time commitments and a lack of transparency. The odds of success for investing in alternatives can be improved if investors have access to premier managers or if talented managers are identified early in their careers.

Anecdotal Observations and Published Opinions

Many professional observers of the markets have shared their insights on manager selection. Research scientists offer valuable advice for practitioners. For example, proponents of the efficient market hypothesis encourage discipline and remind investors to be skeptical of track records and alpha forecasts. Their research suggests investors should look for future opportunities and be wary when "following the crowd." Performance chasing does not work. In other words, do not follow fashion; seek valuation. Empirical research also helps confirm whether commonly held beliefs on investing are valid.

Many research studies report histories of active return cycling and suggest that investors should learn the difference between deep value and relative value portfolio disciplines. Style indices are useful for benchmarking, but it is also important to understand that the beta of a given portfolio, even versus a style index that appears to be relevant, is not necessarily equal to one. Frequently, the strongest performance comes from groups of funds that have recently performed the worst. Consider the situation in which investors have lost patience with their managers. Before deciding to terminate a manager, investors should ask whether they are selling at the bottom. Evidence of the loss of value from manager selection suggests that investors should evaluate their hiring and firing processes, not just their current managers.

Authors of books on pension plans and endowments have shared their experiences after decades of investing. Swensen (2000) reviewed the challenges posed by the principal–agent problem and proposed that investors should be disciplined when implementing investment policy. He noted that relying on past returns is an easy way to make poor investment decisions and that effective management of a portfolio or pool of assets requires hard work and focus on the long term. Olson (2005) observed that little can be learned in a "20–30 minute presentation" other than "which manager is more articulate" (p. 12). His team found it valuable to study portfolio characteristics and manager data to motivate "subjective questions" used in face-to-face meetings.

Ellis (2012) reported on value-destroying behavior by investors: setting unrealistic expectations and the tendency to "buy high, sell low" and "take on higher-volatility managers because their performance looks better" (pp. 13, 14). He also noted that "once the hiring is done, almost nobody involved studies the process" (2012, p. 14). Ellis recommended that investment committees focus on good governance: reviewing staff capabilities, understanding costs, setting clear objectives and short-term risk tolerances, and following guidelines and procedures when implementing investment policy. He also observed that the best investment committees are well trained and "help bring stabilizing, rational consistency" to the process (2012, p. 19). In another paper, Ellis (2011) recommended that institutional investors maintain a stable committee (terms of 5–6 years, renewable once), retain a reasonable number of managers, and aim to achieve an average manager tenure of 10 or more years.

Ronald Peyton (personal communication) of Callan Associates noted that in his experience, the best portfolio managers love investing and making money for their clients and that building trust with managers takes a long time. He observed that poor recent performance from long successful managers represents a buying opportunity, but few investors are willing to accept the career risk of hiring poorly performing managers. Peyton recommended seeking managers who offer a disciplined process with a consistent philosophy and who work in a stable, positive-culture company environment.[96] He noted that a "watch list" can be a useful tool, providing investors with an opportunity to take action in the short term, but can delay the act of termination. In his experience, the best-performing investors are careful to diversify and pursue nothing more than fine-tuning of their asset and manager allocations through time.

Budge Collins (personal communication) of Collins/Bay Island Securities noted that most investors devote their time to studying quantitative data even though the difficult part of selecting managers is the qualitative side. One important goal of qualitative research is to build trust—a process that begins with exhaustive face-to-face meetings, thorough company visits, and extensive reference checks.

Anecdotal observations from portfolio managers suggest several recommendations for selecting superior managers. These include the following:

---

[96]Evidence supporting this recommendation is identified by Groysberg (2010), who found that the success of sell-side research analysts when they move to another firm tends to continue only if they move together as a team.

- Do not be afraid to be away from the crowd, and do not be a permanent bull or bear.

- Ensure that lines of reporting for portfolio managers are client friendly; for example, it is important that the portfolio manager report to the chief investment officer rather than the head of sales.

- Acknowledge that the only way for managers to succeed in the long term is to do something that is unique and cannot be copied. Consider the example of Berkshire Hathaway: The organization follows a very patient process for identifying attractive investments. Others cannot wait like it can.

- Use time with portfolio managers to ask questions that cannot be answered before the meeting or by using published information and that are relevant for alpha generation, portfolio construction, and strategy implementation.

Although this book is intended for use by investors, it also includes insights for managers who want to keep their clients informed and help them avoid mistakes. Ongoing communication, including reminding the client about the mandate's objectives and the portfolio process, is key to developing and maintaining a good relationship. Managers need to set expectations before the strategy is underway if they want to retain their clients through periods of weak results. When performance is weak, managers should redouble their communication efforts. It is helpful to demonstrate that the portfolio is being managed in accordance with established guidelines, explain why recent performance is weak, and point out that strong performance tends to follow periods of underperformance.

Summary Recommendations

Investors, including professionals, often do not follow a well-disciplined investment process. Many hire managers with strong track records instead of managers with strong prospects.

Part-time investors, including individual investors and investment committee members, lack sufficient time to focus on investments because of multiple commitments. They spend what little time they have evaluating tactical decisions and often observe and react to short-term performance volatility. This reaction costs investors billions of dollars annually and leaves little time for strategic or long-term planning.

Realistic investors understand that foolproof systems for successful manager selection do not exist. Noise in the markets limits success, particularly in the short term. Investors can improve their odds by being disciplined, following documented recommendations, and avoiding common mistakes. **Exhibit 10.1** provides a list of broad recommendations.

Exhibit 10.1. Key Recommendations for Effective Manager Selection

1. Formulate a manager selection process and include it in an IPS.

2. Periodically evaluate the success of this process.

3. Do not react to short- and medium-term performance; instead, focus on fundamentals.

4. Understand that certain things are beyond the investor's abilities and control. Continuously improve your knowledge base and skill set.

Know Your Limitations. A good way to begin formulating a manager selection plan is to survey the investor's knowledge and skills. Many investors do not have the training or experience to effectively evaluate a manager's investment process. Security markets are complex, and investment success requires specialization. The time required to become a specialist is significant. Anecdotally, experienced pension consultants may take up to 12 months and conduct many onsite reviews before they are comfortable recommending managers for a new asset class.

Because of the extensive effort required to become an expert in evaluating managers, unskilled investors often rely on readily available performance records, which offer limited value and, in many cases, can lead to mistakes in hiring and firing decisions. Evaluating and improving skills will help investors avoid these common mistakes.

Philosophy and Process. One way for investors to ensure the rigor of their manager selection process is to record both their philosophy and their process regarding manager selection. These statements should be incorporated in an IPS. Mistakes can be avoided by defining objectives, determining a plan to meet those objectives, and assigning responsibilities when appropriate. The investment philosophy should be realistic and reflect the investor's skill set and resources. Questions to consider include the following: How much time does the investor have to monitor his or her investment? Can the investor be skilled at manager timing when he or she is not skilled at market timing? What can the investor expect from a financial adviser or pension consultant? What is the investor's view on active management?

Features of an IPS. As discussed in Chapter 1, an IPS sets the stage for manager selection. The objectives and asset allocation policy outlined in the statement influence the number and type of managers the investor needs to select. An IPS facilitates disciplined manager selection by including guidelines for hiring, monitoring, and terminating managers. The following elements relevant to manager selection can be incorporated in an IPS:

- a list of asset classes to be included in the investment plan, allocations for privately and publicly traded securities, a statement of how the mix satisfies liquidity needs, and instructions for which asset classes will be actively managed versus indexed;

- active risk tolerances and a plan for the distribution of active returns for both individual managers and the plan as a whole;

- a list of knowledge and skills required to support effective manager selection decisions, including specifications for investor training;

- a process for manager selection (described in the following section) for index and active portfolios and privately and publicly traded securities, a list of information needed for hiring and firing decisions, and a list of complementary resources;

- a list of goals for monitoring manager characteristics—both quantitative and qualitative; and

- a requirement to regularly review, validate, and update the process for hiring, reviewing, and terminating managers.

Features of a Manager Search. Articulating the steps required for hiring a manager will improve the investor's chance of success. The following list may be included as an appendix to an IPS:

1. Define goals for the mandate, including active risk.

2. Determine which specialized skills are available and which are needed to select quality managers; draw on the expertise of others if not available in house.

3. Document transaction costs, management fees, and costs of manager turnover, and then determine the level of added value required to cover them; determine the manager's investment capacity and assess his or her commitment to hold assets at that level.

4. Prepare questions to review the manager's philosophy, resources, and culture; articulate a plan for reference checks.

5. Document the manager's investment process; confirm that portfolio characteristics and performance (behavior and attribution) match the stated process.

6. Explore fee arrangements, including details of performance sharing.

7. Define measures of success for the manager and the overall plan; specify the time period for which the manager will be evaluated (the manager should agree with the objectives).

Manager Review. Reacting to performance outliers is ineffective. If investors wait until performance is poor to reduce a manager's allocation, the damage is already done. Moreover, disappointing results may bias investors when conducting reviews of their managers.

Investors should stay informed about their portfolio exposures and their managers' capabilities by conducting regular reviews. Investors should be attuned to warning signs, including changes in manager ownership, reporting responsibilities, personnel roles, resources, staff levels, mindset, and culture.

Final Thoughts

Transaction costs for managing investment plans include the expenses incurred for terminating one manager and hiring another. These costs are not trivial. It is useful to consider, from time to time, what the investor would do if invested 100% in cash. Investors can avoid being biased by inertia if they explore whether they would select the same managers and same weights as they currently hold. If not, it is time to evaluate what it would take to make an adjustment.

Appendix A. The Mathematics of the Arithmetic of Active Management

If active managers closely represent the entire market, then on average, their performance, gross of fees and transaction costs, should be close to the market averages. Either lucky or superior managers will outperform the averages and either unlucky or inferior managers will underperform. If highly skilled managers can generate value net of costs and expenses, then the search for this skill may be a worthwhile endeavor, but if future alpha is highly variable and the observable determinants of skill offer only minimal predictive power, this endeavor may not pay off—hence, the conundrum of selecting active managers.

Articulating the arithmetic of active management is relatively straightforward. Assume the market is made up of N portfolios, for which the asset size is known for each at the beginning of the period.[97] Let

P_i = beginning-of-period market weight of portfolio i (assets of portfolio i divided by total assets in market) such that $\Sigma_i P_i = 1$,

S_{ik} = beginning-of-period weight of security k within portfolio i,

W_k = beginning-of-period market-cap weight of security k in the market,

R_k = period return on security k, and

rp_i = period return on portfolio i.

Then, market return is $R_M = \Sigma_k W_k R_k$. Substituting $\Sigma_k P_i S_{ik}$ for W_k, market return can be decomposed and reconstituted as follows:

$$R_M = \Sigma_k W_k R_k = \Sigma_i \Sigma_k P_i S_{ik} R_k = \Sigma_i P_i rp_i. \tag{A1}$$

This equation confirms that the overall market return is simply the sum of asset-weighted portfolio returns. Of course, it is based on the assumption that all portfolios are included in the calculations. Note that the mean portfolio return, defined in Equation A2, is simply a function of the number of portfolios, N, independent of the asset levels of the portfolios:

$$\frac{\Sigma_i \Sigma_k S_{ik} R_i}{N} = \frac{\Sigma_i rp_i}{N}. \tag{A2}$$

As a result, no conclusion about the value of active management can be drawn from comparing estimates of the values of the left and right sides of Equation A1 published in the marketplace. If they are not equal, it is because not all portfolios are included in the calculation (or portfolio returns are not gross of costs). There is also no value in comparing R_M with the mean portfolio return (Equation A2). The two expressions will be equal only if every portfolio is identical in asset size.

---

[97]This derivation is based on that used in holdings-based performance decomposition. See Stewart, Heisler, and Piros (2011).

Appendix B. The Mathematics of Optimal Asset Allocation

Determining optimal asset allocation requires studying asset class returns and, in many cases, how returns behave relative to financial liabilities. If the assumption is that all investors have the same utility function and markets are liquid and fully efficient, they will all hold the same portfolio—the market portfolio, which includes all assets. But if investors have heterogeneous views on the future or exhibit heterogeneous utility functions, they will choose different total portfolios. Once investors' portfolio strategies are formulated, they will implement them by hiring managers to run part or all of them. Investors typically select one or more managers for each asset class.

Ideally, optimal manager selection and asset allocation should be accomplished in a single step that incorporates the investor's views on and the relationship between manager alphas and asset class returns. A common formula for computing utility from risk and return is the single-period, mean–variance, constant relative risk aversion expression, show in Equation B1:[98]

$$E(\text{Utility}_S) = E(R) - \lambda_S \sigma^2(R). \tag{B1}$$

Investors seek higher expected return, $E(R)$, and lower risk, $\sigma^2(R)$. The relative importance of these two factors is determined by a risk aversion parameter, λ_S. Risk includes both systematic and residual risk, and it can be reduced by lowering total portfolio beta, increasing asset and manager diversification, and weighting low-residual-risk managers more heavily. Optimal asset class weights can be set by optimizing the function by using a quadratic optimizer with constraints on weights and other targets. The higher the level of λ_S, with all else being constant, the lower the optimal portfolio's risk.

In practice, institutional investors do not select both asset allocations and managers in one step. They tend to select managers after setting strategic asset allocations. As a result, asset allocation and manager selection reflect different types of risk aversion. This subject is discussed further in Chapter 5.

The utility function listed in Equation B1 incorporates total returns, either nominal or real, but many investors focus on their cash flow needs, such as pension benefit payments. In these cases, the utility function must consider the difference in returns between the assets and the liability. The following equation specifies a return on assets (R) and a return on the liability (R_L):

$$E(\text{Utility}_L) = E(R - R_L) - \lambda_L \sigma^2(R - R_L). \tag{B2}$$

---

[98]See Stewart et al. (2011) for the development of this approach.

In practice, most liabilities have characteristics similar to those of bonds (although they are negatives on the balance sheet). As a result, optimizers favor fixed-income assets and managers to reduce the risk of asset/liability mismatch. It is common for investors to choose managers who can build customized bond portfolios to meet their real or nominal cash flow needs or at least match the duration of their liabilities.

Both of these utility frameworks assume a single-period world; they assume that investors set their asset weights and retain them for the entire investment horizon. The frameworks are very helpful in practice but are not valid theoretically when changes in economic parameters—including risk, return, and preferences—occur. Dynamic asset allocation optimization techniques incorporate changing parameters and can help determine how allocations should be adjusted over time.[99] Some techniques—for example, portfolio insurance—incorporate current versus target asset levels. Others, such as shortfall probability techniques, recognize that risk changes as horizons shorten. Dynamic optimization problems are commonly solved backward—that is, a series of single-period optimization problems is solved beginning with the final period. Simulation tools can also be used to solve dynamic problems. One key benefit of using dynamic models is that they provide a path for investors to follow through time. Manager selection is influenced by the degree of change in allocations through time. Significant changes in allocations lead investors to prefer managers who offer liquidity.

Single-period utility optimization tools for setting portfolio weights are described in Chapter 5. The utility functions within those tools incorporate active return mean and variance in place of total return mean and variance. The reason is that asset allocation is assumed to be constant when determining portfolio allocations. Dynamic manager selection issues are also discussed in Chapter 5 and 6.

---

[99]See Stewart et al. (2011) for a detailed summary of these techniques.

Appendix C. The Mathematics of Optimal Manager Allocation

Setting the optimal allocation of investment managers incorporates equations from Chapters 3, 4, and 5 and is straightforward under the assumption of a single-factor risk model with independently distributed alpha and error terms. Recall the following equation (C1) that decomposes the total return on a given portfolio. A portfolio's total return is defined by rp, its beta by β_p, and its error term by ep. The t (time) subscripts have been omitted. Note that the alpha term can be zero (index fund) or nonzero (active fund). We can make the model more interesting by assuming that alpha (α) is a random variable with a nonzero mean, independent of the market and error term (which has a zero mean).

$$rp = \alpha_p + R_f + \beta_p \left(R_M - R_f \right) + ep. \tag{C1}$$

Define rs as the return on the investor's total strategic portfolio implemented with a combination of individual portfolios. It is the return on the weighted sum of the underlying portfolios each weighted by ws_j (the weight of each manager j) and can be expressed as

$$rs = \sum_j ws_j rp_j = \sum_j ws_j \left[\alpha_{Pj} + R_f + \beta_{Pj} \left(R_M - R_f \right) + ep_j \right]. \tag{C2}$$

The total portfolio's benchmark's return, rb, is shown in Equation C3. Note that alphas are omitted because the benchmark is composed of indices, not live portfolios. The benchmark beta does not necessarily equal one; the investor can choose weights different from those represented by market capitalizations.[100] Each live portfolio j has its own benchmark index j, but benchmark (wb) and live total portfolio (ws) weights do not necessarily match.

$$rb = \sum_j wb_j ri_j = \sum_j wb_j \left[R_f + \beta_{Ij} \left(R_M - R_f \right) + ei_j \right]. \tag{C3}$$

The goal of the investor is to set the weights, ws_j, of the individual live portfolios to yield the optimal implementation of the total benchmark portfolio. As a result, the focus is on active return as shown in the following:

$$rs - rb = \sum_j ws_j rp_j - \sum_j wb_j ri_j \tag{C4}$$

$$= \sum_j ws_j \alpha_{Pj} + \sum_j \left(ws_j \beta_{Pj} - wb_j \beta_{Ij} \right) \left(R_M - R_f \right) \tag{C5}$$

$$+ \sum_j \left(ws_j ep_j - wb_j ei_j \right).$$

---

[100]Note that the total market, including nontradable assets, may not be investable.

Formulas for expected return and variance are shown in the following equations. Assuming weights sum to one and residual return (including alpha) components are uncorrelated, the expected return and variance of active return for the overall live portfolio can be expressed as

$$E(rs - rb) = \sum_j ws_j E(\alpha_{Pj}) + \sum_j (ws_j \beta_{Pj} - wb_j \beta_{Ij})[E(R_M) - R_f]; \quad \text{(C6)}$$

$$\sigma^2(rs - rb) = \sum_j ws_j^2 \sigma^2(\alpha_{Pj}) + \sum_j (ws_j \beta_{Pj} - wb_j \beta_{Ij})^2 \sigma^2(R_M)$$
$$+ \sum_j (ws - wb_j)^2 \sigma^2(ep_j - ei_j). \quad \text{(C7)}$$

The expected active return on the live portfolio includes two terms: the weighted average expected alpha and the difference in weighted beta exposures multiplied by the expected market excess return over the risk-free rate. Stated differently, expected active return equals expected alpha plus the expected return from beta misfit. The active return variance term includes three components: the weighted (by the sum of weights squared) variance of alpha, the weighted (by active weights) beta exposures (squared and summed) times the market return variance, and the weighted (by the sum of squared active weights) variance of the difference in error terms.[101] In other words, risk depends on alpha exposure weighted by alpha volatility, beta mismatch weighted by market volatility, and a measure of weighted active residual risk.

As introduced in Chapter 5, assuming the investor's utility function is of common quadratic form, the expected utility of active return can be specified as follows:

$$E(U) = E(rs - rb) - \lambda \sigma^2(rs - rb), \quad \text{(C8)}$$

where λ is a constant measure of active return risk aversion.

The investor's utility is determined by expected active return minus risk aversion times risk, where risk is defined as active return variance. The risk aversion parameter (λ) expresses the relative importance of active return and risk to a particular investor. A higher value of λ means that the investor dislikes risk to a greater extent.

The solution to an investor's manager selection problem is to identify the manager weights that provide the highest utility. A requirement that weights are positive and sum to 100% are common constraints. Other options include constraining the probability of a given level of underperformance (downside constraint).

Alternatively, an investor may be comfortable accepting a given level of risk defined in terms of standard deviation (B_g), downside risk (loss of

---

[101]Note that the three risk terms can be separated because of the assumption of independence between the return components.

percentage D_p or more at percentage probability P_p), or value at risk (a form of downside risk but valued in dollars D_V at percentage probability P_V). These different approaches can be specified mathematically as follows:

1. Maximize utility:

$$\text{Maximize } E(rs - rb) - \lambda\sigma^2(rs - rb), \tag{C9}$$

$$\text{subject to } \begin{matrix} \Sigma_j\, ws_j = 1.0; \\ ws_j \geq 0.0. \end{matrix}$$

2. Risk budget to control active return standard deviation:

$$\text{Maximize } E(rs - rb), \tag{C10}$$

$$\text{subject to } \begin{matrix} \Sigma_j\, ws_j = 1.0; \\ ws_j \geq 0.0; \\ \sigma(rs - rb) \leq B_S. \end{matrix}$$

A risk budget can be specified by using measures of risk other than standard deviation by replacing the last term σ with either of the following:

-   downside risk of losing percentage D_p or more, referred to as probability P_p:

    $$\text{Probability}[(rs - rb) \leq D_P] \leq P_P.$$

-   value at risk (VaR)[102] dollar target D_V, at tail probability P_V, at dollar value of assets \$X:

    $$\left[\text{VaR}(rs - rb)\middle|\$X, P_V\right] \leq D_V.$$

An investor can also choose to control the portfolio's beta to match the benchmark's beta by adding a further constraint, as follows:

$$\Sigma_j\left(ws_j\beta_{Pj} - wb_j\beta_{Ij}\right) = 0. \tag{C11}$$

An investor can choose to minimize active risk altogether and focus solely on selecting the lowest-risk mix of portfolios. In that case, there will be no maximization, only minimization of active risk:

$$\text{Minimize } \sigma^2(rs - rb), \tag{C12}$$

$$\text{subject to } \begin{matrix} \Sigma_j\, ws_j = 1.0; \\ ws_j \geq 0.0. \end{matrix}$$

In practice, investors can use a standard optimization tool, such as Solver in Excel, to solve this problem, as illustrated in Appendix E. Of course, an

---

[102]VaR is defined in Appendix D.

investor would need to specify a risk aversion parameter and provide expected total returns and alphas and a variance/covariance matrix of total returns, alphas, and residual returns for the problem. Investors may want to run several scenarios using different formulations and assumed values to develop a feel for the influence of different assumptions on the optimal solution.

It is also recommended that investors study historical return patterns. This research should include computing the frequency of active returns within particular ranges, the size and length of periods of poor performance, the timing and size of performance subsequent to unusually strong or weak performance, and general patterns of cyclicality.

As discussed in Chapter 5, investors tend to select strategic asset class weights and manager weights in separate steps, usually setting asset allocation before setting manager allocation. Another way to build a portfolio of managers is to select weights for alphas without being constrained by strategic allocation. Investors can select the best managers regardless of asset class and use derivatives to adjust asset allocation to match the strategic allocation. Piros (1998) proposed this approach and noted that "as the relative attractiveness of various asset classes changes over time there is no need to forgo the value-added generated by the most skilled managers just because their asset class is out of favor" (p. 3).[103] One caveat is that derivatives, including swaps, warrants, and futures, all involve fees and transaction costs, so the alpha calculations must be computed net of hedging expenses.

As mentioned in Appendix B, allocation optimization can be conducted by assuming either single or multiple periods. The expressions listed in this appendix reflect a single-period world where optimal allocations are fixed for the entire horizon and are realistic only if market parameters and investor preferences are fixed. Dynamic optimization (namely, dynamic programming or optimal control) techniques also exist and can be used as an alternative to the single-period method described here.

---

[103]Also see Clarke, de Silva, and Thorley (2009).

Appendix D. Definitions of Optimization Parameters

These definitions are presented in Stewart et al. (2011). Define theta (θ) as the return value R that investors do not want to be lower than and P as the probability that the realized return will be equal to or less than that value. If returns are arranged in ascending order (the i associated with the lowest possible value is 1), we can define K to denote the largest integer such that $R(K) \leq \theta$. Downside probability is given by

$$\text{Downside probability} = \sum_1^K P(i). \tag{D1}$$

A downside probability of 5% can be interpreted as a 5% chance that returns will equal θ or less. A value of zero is commonly used for θ.

The lower partial moment (LPM) is the sum of deviations (taken to the power of degree n) of returns below a threshold level. The LPM of degree "2" with threshold return θ and probability P is

$$
\begin{aligned}
\text{LPM} &= \sum_1^N P(i)\left\{\max\left[0, \theta - R(i)\right]\right\}^2 \\
&= \sum_1^K P(i)\left[\theta - R(i)\right]^2.
\end{aligned}
\tag{D2}
$$

If θ is set equal to the expected return, the LPM is also known as the semi-variance.

Value at risk (VaR) is a measure of risk expressed in currency value (such as the number of dollars at risk) rather than percentage return. Both the size of the exposure and the probability of a given loss must be computed to determine VaR. The common interpretation is a given dollar loss (the value that is at risk) or lower that has a stated chance of occurring.[104] Let $CP(k) = \sum_1^k P(i)$ be the cumulative probability for the k lowest return values, and R is return. Let L be the largest value of k such that $CP(L) \leq TP$, a target probability of loss. As a result, $R(L)$ is the (highest) return at the top of the outcomes in the left tail of the distribution. For an investment of X and a tail probability of TP, the VaR equals $XR(L)$. That is,

$$\text{VaR}(X, TP) = XR(L) \tag{D3}$$

for L such that $CP(L) \leq TP$.

---

[104]VaR is frequently understood to be the amount that can be lost. This interpretation is flawed; as mentioned in the text, it is that amount or more, *not* that amount or less.

©2013 The Research Foundation of CFA Institute

Note that VaR is only meaningful if TP is chosen such that $R(L) < 0$ (i.e., a loss). Typically, $TP = 0.05$, implying that a loss of VaR *or more* occurs 5% of the time. As a result, the actual loss may be (or perhaps probably will be) worse than VaR.

Appendix E. Excel

Excel, Part 1. The following screen shot shows a template that can be used to compute optimal mixes of funds and is the source of the information displayed in Table 5.1. The template is divided into two sections: inputs (TOTAL RETURNS) and outputs (ACTIVE RETURNS). Cells C5 through F5 include weights of individual funds, and G5 is the total [=SUM(C5:F5)]. The cells in columns C through I beginning in row 7 are populated with 10 years of monthly returns beginning in October 2001 (shown as 200110). Cell I7 includes a formula to calculate the weighted average of fund returns (+$C$5*C7+$D$5*D7+$E$5*E7+$F$5*F7), which is copied through row 126.

	A	B	C	D	E	F	G	H	I
1		**TOTAL RETURNS**							
2			Index Fund	Value Fund	Growth Fund	Core Fund	Index	1 month Risk Free	Combined Portfolio of Funds
3									
4							TOTAL		
5	**WEIGHTS**		0	0	0	1	1		
6		Month							
7		200110	0.057364	0.0415	0.10707	0.060631	0.063643	0.0022	0.060631
8		200111	0.065899	0.0635	0.071325	0.100724	0.070591	0.0017	0.100724
9		200112	0.066613	0.0534	0.057247	0.088763	0.062348	0.0015	0.088763

Cell J7 (five cells below Active Return vs. Index in the section ACTIVE RETURNS) includes a formula to calculate active return (+I7−G7), and Cell L3 provides the standard deviation of monthly active returns [=STDEV(J7:J126)]. Cell L4 is the mean active return [=AVERAGE(J7:J126)], and Cell L5 is the annualized standard deviation [=(((L3^2+(1+L4)^2))^12-(1+L4)^24)^0.5]. Excess returns of the portfolio and of the benchmark index, over the risk-free rate, are needed to calculate beta. These begin in Row 7 of columns N (beginning with the formula +I7−H7 and copied down) and O (beginning with the formula +G7−H7). The formula for a single-factor beta is in Cell O3 [=SLOPE(N7:N126,O7:O126)]. Cumulative returns are in columns P [beginning with =(1+I7)*P6 in row 7 (with row 6 value of 1.0) and copied down] and Q [beginning with =(1+G7)*Q6]. The active 12-month return is computed in column R (not shown in the screen shot). It begins in row 18 with the formula (+P18/P6)−(Q18/Q6) and is copied down to row 126.

J	K	L	M	N	O	P	Q	R	S	T
ACTIVE RETURNS					**COMPUTATIONS**					
Active Return vs. Index		Active Return Descriptive Statistics		Beta		Ann. Comb. Port. Return	Ann. Index Return	Ann. Active Return	Frequency ≤ Downside	Utility
	std dev	0.017547			**0.906**	0.087	0.076	0.011	51.4%	0.00375
	mean	0.00071						12 Month		
	ann sd	**0.06131**		rp – rf	rm – rf	Cum Ret	Cum Idx	Active	Downside	
						1	1		0	
-0.003012				0.058431	0.061443	1.060631	1.063643			
0.030134				0.099024	0.068891	1.167462	1.138726			
0.026414				0.087263	0.060848	1.271089	1.209724			

Utility is defined as expected active return (the historical mean in this example) minus risk (historical variance) times a risk aversion parameter. It is provided in Cell T3 with the formula =+R3-2*L5^2 (risk aversion is assumed to be 2 in this example but can be easily changed). The frequency of annual active returns below a target value is generated in Cell S3 with the formula =SUM(S18:S126)/ COUNT(S18:S126). Column S includes the "if" statement =IF(R18<$S$6,1,0) in rows 18 through 126, which returns the value 1 if the active return is less than the parameter set in Cell S6 under the heading <u>Downside</u> and 0 otherwise.

Once the data and formulas are entered, the spreadsheet can be used to compute optimal portfolios of funds based on expected active return, risk, and utility. The spreadsheet uses historical data to estimate expected return (based on the mean historical return) and risk (based on historical standard deviation). In practice, the spreadsheet can be customized to incorporate exogenous active return and risk estimates.

As an example, consider a portfolio that offers the maximum level of utility. Open the Solver feature in Excel, set the target cell to T3, and click "Max" to set up the objective function. Be sure to include the weights C5:F5 as the cells to change in order to find the optimal value of the objective function. To ensure weights are all greater than zero and sum to 100%, add two constraints: "C5:F5 >= 0" and "G5 = 1". Click "Solve" for the solution. The optimizer will yield the maximum-utility portfolio summarized in Table 5.1.

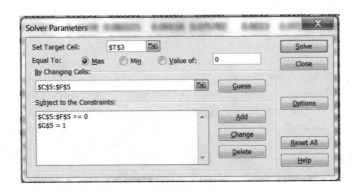

The solution will look like the following:

	A	B	C	D	E	F	G	H	I
1		**TOTAL RETURNS**							
2			Index Fund	Value Fund	Growth Fund	Core Fund	Index	1 month Risk Free	Combined Portfolio of Funds
3									
4							TOTAL		
5	**WEIGHTS**		0	0.396733	0	0.603267	1		

	J	K	L	M	N	O	P	Q	R	S	T
	ACTIVE RETURNS					**COMPUTATIONS**					
	Active Return vs. Index		Active Return Descriptive Statistics			Beta	Ann. Comb. Port. Return	Ann. Index Return	Ann. Active Return	Frequency ≤ Downside	Utility
		std dev	0.014664			0.878	0.088	0.076	0.012	50.5%	0.00642
		mean	0.00060						12 Month		
		ann sd	0.05117		rp - rf	rm - rf	Cum Ret	Cum Idx	Active	Downside	
							1	1		0	

Note that beta is not equal to one, so the solution will be biased to under-perform in up markets. To address this issue, an additional constraint requiring beta (provided in Cell O3) to equal one can be added to the Solver setup.

It can be tempting to control the frequency of underperformance. Because the cells computing frequency in this spreadsheet include an "if" statement, the optimization problem will require an "integer" solution that cannot be accessed in standard Excel. One way to address this issue is to assume a probability distribution (such as normal) and calculate the downside probability (or partial moments) using the assumed distribution instead of the realized series of active returns displayed in the spreadsheet.

Excel, Part 2. The following screen shot is an Excel template that estimates historical alpha by using a four-factor linear equity model. This technique is used to generate the information displayed in Table 6.2. The dependent variable in the regression model consists of the values in column C, which represents the excess return (total return minus the risk-free rate, Rf) of the portfolio. The independent variables include a market index excess return and three additional factor returns: SMB (small-cap minus large-cap stock returns), HML (value minus growth) as defined by Fama and French (1993), and MOM (a measure of momentum defined by high-past-return stocks minus low-past-return stocks) as defined by Carhart (1997). Factor returns for several global equity markets are available at Kenneth French's website (http://mba.tuck.dartmouth.edu/pages/faculty/ken.french/data_library.html).

	A	B	C	D	E	F	G
1	Year	Portfolio	Portfolio - Rf	Index - Rf	SMB	HML	MOM
2	200110	6.10%	5.88	2.58	6.83	-6.99	-8.42
3	200111	10.11%	9.94	7.7	0.39	0.82	-8.62
4	200112	8.92%	8.77	1.63	5.12	0.39	0.01
5	200201	0.61%	0.47	-1.74	1.15	3.46	3.73
6	200202	-1.05%	-1.18	-2.3	-1.67	3.92	6.81
7	200203	9.16%	9.03	4.34	4.34	1.14	-1.68

To estimate a portfolio's alpha relative to the market and adjusted for factor exposures, select "regression" in "data analysis." The window shown in the following screen shot will appear. In this example, 10 years of monthly data are reflected in 120 rows, beginning in row 2. The "Y Range" is the dependent variable. Select column C for the Y Range and columns D through G as the "X Range" (the independent variables). The output provides estimates of the intercept (alpha) and the coefficients (factor exposures or betas) as well as measures of statistical significance, illustrated in the picture with "SUMMARY OUTPUT" at the top. Note that the alpha is a monthly number that can be annualized by multiplying by 12. As mentioned in the text, if the portfolio's benchmark is not the S&P 500, running a second regression for the benchmark and a study of the differences between the two sets of estimates is recommended.

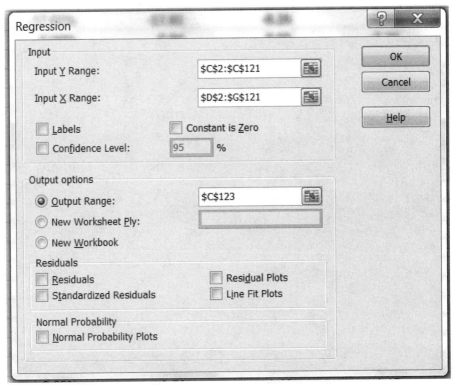

SUMMARY OUTPUT

Regression Statistics	
Multiple R	0.959527624
R Square	0.92069326
Adjusted R Square	0.917934765
Standard Error	1.555291485
Observations	120

ANOVA

	df	SS	MS	F	Significance F
Regression	4	3229.433139	807.3582847	333.766479	2.76847E-62
Residual	115	278.1771345	2.418931605		
Total	119	3507.610273			

	Coefficients	Standard Error	t Stat	P-value	Lower 95%
Intercept	0.105189391	0.144288567	0.72902097	0.46747095	-0.180618482
X Variable 1	0.903079016	0.036660658	24.63346479	1.09276E-47	0.830461312
X Variable 2	0.741572555	0.05945026	12.47383207	4.16589E-23	0.623813036
X Variable 3	0.080799612	0.056224796	1.437081457	0.153410068	-0.030570885
X Variable 4	0.067083971	0.029088682	2.306188066	0.022891588	0.009464893

BIBLIOGRAPHY

Ackermann, Carl, Richard McEnnaly, and David Ravenscraft. 1999. "The Performance of Hedge Funds: Risk, Return and Incentives." *Journal of Finance*, vol. 54, no. 3 (June):833–874.

Agarwal, Prasun. 2007. "Institutional Ownership and Stock Liquidity." Working paper, Cornell University (November).

Agarwal, Vikas, Naveen Daniel, and Narayan Naik. 2009. "Role of Managerial Incentives and Discretion in Hedge Fund Performance." *Journal of Finance*, vol. 64, no. 5 (October):2221–2256.

Andonov, Aleksandar, Rob M.M.J. Bauer, and K.J. Martijn Cremers. 2011. "Can Large Pension Funds Beat the Market? Asset Allocation, Market Timing, Security Selection and the Limits of Liquidity." Working paper, Maastricht University (October).

Baks, Klaas P., Andrew Metrick, and Jessica Wachter. 2001. "Should Investors Avoid All Actively Managed Mutual Funds? A Study in Bayesian Performance Evaluation." *Journal of Finance*, vol. 56, no. 1 (February):45–85.

Barber, Brad, T. Odean, and L. Zheng. 2005. "Out of Sight, Out of Mind: The Effects of Expenses on Mutual Fund Flows." *Journal of Business*, vol. 78, no. 6 (November):2095–2120.

Barras, Laurent, Olivier Scaillet, and Russ Wermers. 2010. "False Discoveries in Mutual Fund Performance: Measuring Luck in Estimated Alphas." *Journal of Finance*, vol. 65, no. 1 (February):179–216.

Bauer, Rob M.M.J., K.J. Martijn Cremers, and Rik G.P. Frehen. 2010. "Pension Fund Performance and Costs: Small Is Beautiful." Yale International Center for Finance Working Paper 10-04 (29 April).

Bauer, Rob, Kees Koedijk, and Rogér Otten. 2005. "International Evidence on Ethical Mutual Fund Performance and Investment Style." *Journal of Banking & Finance*, vol. 29, no. 1 (July):1751–1767.

Baum, J.R., and E.A. Locke. 2004. "The Relationship of Entrepreneurial Traits, Skill, and Motivation to Subsequent Venture Growth." *Journal of Applied Psychology*, vol. 89, no. 4 (August):587–598.

Bergstresser, Daniel, John Chalmers, and Peter Tufano. 2009. "Assessing the Costs and Benefits of Brokers in the Mutual Fund Industry." *Review of Financial Studies*, vol. 22, no. 10 (October):4129–4156.

Bhardwaj, Geetesh, Gary B. Gorton, and K. Geert Rouwenhorst. 2008. "Fooling Some of the People All of the Time: The Inefficient Performance and Persistence of Commodity Trading Advisors." Yale International Center of Finance Working Paper 08-21 (October).

Blake, David, and Allan Timmermann. 1998. "Mutual Fund Performance: Evidence from the UK." *European Finance Review*, vol. 2, no. 1 (June):57–77.

Bodie, Zvi, Alex Kane, and Alan Marcus. 2010. *Investments*. 9th ed. New York: McGraw-Hill.

Bond, Shaun, and Paul Mitchell. 2010. "Alpha and Persistence in Real Estate Fund Performance." *Journal of Real Estate Finance and Economics*, vol. 41, no. 1 (July):53–79.

Brinson, Gary, and Nimrod Fachler. 1985. "Measuring Non-U.S. Equity Portfolio Performance." *Journal of Portfolio Management*, vol. 11, no. 3 (Spring):73–76.

Brown, Stephen, and William Goetzmann. 1995. "Performance Persistence." *Journal of Finance*, vol. 50, no. 2 (June):679–698.

Brown, Stephen, William Goetzmann, and Bing Liang. 2003. "Fees on Fees in Funds of Funds." NBER Working Paper 9464 (February).

Buffett, Warren. 2001. "Warren Buffett: A Conversation with Dean Cynthia H. Milligan." *Nebraska Business* (Fall).

Busse, J.A., A. Goyal, and S. Wahal. 2010. "Performance and Persistence in Institutional Investment Management." *Journal of Finance*, vol. 65, no. 2 (April):765–790.

Carhart, Mark. 1997. "On Persistence in Mutual Fund Performance." *Journal of Finance*, vol. 52, no. 1 (March):57–82.

Chen, Honghui, Gregory Noronha, and Vijay Singal. 2006. "Index Changes and Losses to Index Fund Investors." *Financial Analysts Journal*, vol. 62, no. 4 (July/August):31–47.

Chevalier, Judith, and Glenn Ellison. 1997. "Risk Taking by Mutual Funds as a Response to Incentives." *Journal of Political Economy*, vol. 105, no. 6 (December):1167–1200.

———. 1999. "Are Some Mutual Fund Managers Better than Others? Cross-Sectional Patterns in Behavior and Performance." *Journal of Finance*, vol. 54, no. 3 (June):875–899.

Clarke, Roger G., Harindra de Silva, and Steven Thorley. 2009. *Investing Separately in Alpha and Beta*. Charlottesville, VA: Research Foundation of CFA Institute.

Coleman, Thomas S. 2011. *A Practical Guide to Risk Management*. Charlottesville, VA: Research Foundation of CFA Institute.

DALBAR. 2005. "Quantitative Analysis of Investor Behavior 2005."

Davanzo, Lawrence E., and Stephen L. Nesbitt. 1987. "Performance Fees for Investment Performance." *Financial Analysts Journal*, vol. 43, no. 1 (January/February):14–20.

Davis, E. Philip. 2005. "Pension Fund Management and International Investment—A Global Perspective." *Pensions International Journal*, vol. 10, no. 3 (June):236–261.

Del Guercio, Diane, and Paula A. Tkac. 2002. "The Determinants of the Flow of Funds of Managed Portfolios: Mutual Funds versus Pension Funds." *Journal of Financial and Quantitative Analysis*, vol. 37, no. 4 (December):523–557.

Driebusch, Corrie. 2013. "Your Fund Is a Laggard. Should You Sell?" *Wall Street Journal* (4 February):R7.

Ellis, Charles. 2011. "Best Practice Investment Committees." *Journal of Portfolio Management*, vol. 37, no. 2 (Winter):139–147.

———. 2012. "Murder on the Orient Express: The Mystery of Underperformance." *Financial Analysts Journal*, vol. 68, no. 4 (July/August):13–19.

Elton, Edwin J., Martin Gruber, and Christopher Blake. 2003. "Incentive Fees and Mutual Funds." *Journal of Finance*, vol. 58, no. 2 (April):779–804.

Elton, Edwin J., Martin J. Gruber, and Jeffrey A. Busse. 2004. "Are Investors Rational? Choices among Index Funds." *Journal of Finance*, vol. 59, no. 1 (February):261–288.

Evans, Allison. 2008. "Portfolio Manager Ownership and Mutual Fund Performance." *Financial Management*, vol. 37, no. 3 (Autumn):513–534.

Fama, Eugene F., and Kenneth R. French. 1993. "Common Risk Factors in the Returns on Stocks and Bonds." *Journal of Financial Economics*, vol. 33, no. 1 (February):3–56.

———. 2010. "Luck versus Skill in the Cross-Section of Mutual Fund Returns." *Journal of Finance*, vol. 65, no. 5 (October):1915–1947.

Fama, Eugene F., and Robert Litterman. 2012. "An Experienced View on Markets and Investing." *Financial Analysts Journal*, vol. 68, no. 6 (November/December):15–19.

Farnsworth, H., and J. Taylor. 2006. "Evidence on the Compensation of Portfolio Managers." *Journal of Financial Research*, vol. 29, no. 3 (Fall):305–324.

Forbes, Kristin. 2010. "Why Do Foreigners Invest in the United States?" *Journal of International Economics*, vol. 80, no. 1 (January):3–21.

Foster, F. Douglas, and Geoffrey Warren. 2013. "Equity Manager Selection and Portfolio Formation: Interviews with Investment Staff." Financial Research Network (FIRN) Research Papers, vol. 2, no. 2 (3 May).

———. Forthcoming. "Why Might Investors Choose Active Management?" *Journal of Behavioral Finance.*

Frazzini, Andrea, and Owen Lamont. 2008. "Dumb Money: Mutual Fund Flows and the Cross-Section of Stock Returns." *Journal of Financial Economics*, vol. 88, no. 2 (May):299–322.

French, Kenneth. 2008. "Presidential Address: The Cost of Active Investing." *Journal of Finance*, vol. 63, no. 4 (August):1537–1573.

Fung, William, David Hsieh, Narayan Naik, and Tarun Ramadorai. 2008. "Hedge Funds: Performance, Risk, and Capital Formation." *Journal of Finance*, vol. 63, no. 4 (August):1777–1803.

Gemmill, Gordon, and Dylan Thomas. 2006. "The Impact of Corporate Governance on Closed-End Funds." *European Financial Management*, vol. 12, no. 5:725–746.

Gil-Bazo, Javier, and Pablo Ruiz-Verdú. 2009. "The Relation between Price and Performance in the Mutual Fund Industry." *Journal of Finance*, vol. 64, no. 5 (October):2153–2183.

Golec, J.H. 1996. "The Effects of Mutual Funds Managers' Characteristics on Their Portfolio Performance, Risk and Fees." *Financial Services Review*, vol. 5, no. 2:133–147.

Goleman, Daniel. 1998. "What Makes a Leader?" *Harvard Business Review*, vol. 82, no. 1 (January):82–91. Reprinted January 2004.

Gottesman, Aron, and Matthew Morey. 2006. "Manager Education and Mutual Fund Performance." *Journal of Empirical Finance*, vol. 13, no. 1 (March):145–182.

Goyal, Amit, and Sunil Wahal. 2008. "The Selection and Termination of Investment Management Firms by Plan Sponsors." *Journal of Finance*, vol. 63, no. 4 (August):1805–1847.

Grinold, Richard, and Ronald Kahn. 2000. *Active Portfolio Management*. 2nd ed. New York: McGraw-Hill.

Grinold, Richard, and Andrew Rudd. 1987. "Incentive Fees: Who Wins? Who Loses?" *Financial Analysts Journal*, vol. 43, no. 1 (January/February):27–38.

Grossman, Sanford. 1995. "Dynamic Asset Allocation and the Informational Efficiency of Markets." *Journal of Finance*, vol. 50, no. 3 (July):773–1027.

Grossman, Sanford, and Joseph Stiglitz. 1980. "On the Impossibility of Informationally Efficient Markets." *American Economic Review*, vol. 70, no. 3 (June):393–408.

Groysberg, Boris. 2010. *Chasing Stars: The Myth of Talent and the Portability of Performance*. Princeton, NJ: Princeton University Press.

Gruber, Martin J. 1996. "Another Puzzle: The Growth in Actively Managed Mutual Funds." *Journal of Finance*, vol. 51, no. 3 (July):783–810.

Hayek, F.A. 1945. "The Use of Knowledge in Society." *American Economic Review*, vol. 35, no. 4 (September):519–530.

Heisler, Jeffrey, Christopher R. Knittel, John J. Neumann, and Scott D. Stewart. 2007. "Why Do Institutional Plan Sponsors Hire and Fire Their Investment Managers?" *Journal of Business and Economic Studies*, vol. 13, no. 1 (Spring):88–115.

Hernández, Cesar, and Scott Stewart. 2001. "Overseas Equity Managers Are Not as Consistent as US Equity Managers." Working paper, Fidelity Investments.

ICI. 2006. "Mutual Funds and Institutional Accounts: A Comparison." Investment Company Institute (26 January).

———. 2008. "2008 Investment Company Fact Book." 48th ed. Investment Company Institute (14 May).

———. 2012. "2012 Investment Company Fact Book." 52nd ed. Investment Company Institute (2 May).

———. 2013. "2013 Investment Company Fact Book." 53rd ed. Investment Company Institute (20 April).

Jagannathan, Ravi, Alexey Malakhov, and Dmitry Novikov. 2010. "Do Hot Hands Exist among Hedge Fund Managers? An Empirical Evaluation." *Journal of Finance*, vol. 65, no. 1 (February):217–255.

Jarrow, Robert. 2010. "Active Portfolio Management and Positive Alphas: Fact or Fantasy?" *Journal of Portfolio Management*, vol. 36, no. 2 (Winter):17–22.

Javadekar, Apoorva. 2012. "New Methodology Regression." Unpublished manuscript, Boston University.

Jensen, Michael. 1968. "The Performance of Mutual Funds in the Period 1945–1964." *Journal of Finance*, vol. 23, no. 2 (May):389–416.

Kang, Qiang, Xi Li, and Tie Su. 2011. "CFA Certification Program and Sell-Side Analysts." Working paper, University of Miami (March).

Kaplan, Steven, and Antoinette Schoar. 2005. "Private Equity Performance: Returns, Persistence, and Capital Flows." *Journal of Finance*, vol. 60, no. 4 (August):1791–1823.

Karim, S., and S. Stewart. 2004. "Summary of Survey of Decision Making by Public and Corporate Pension Professionals." Unpublished presentation manuscript, Boston University.

Khorana, Ajay, Henri Servaes, and Peter Tufano. 2009. "Mutual Fund Fees around the World." *Review of Financial Studies*, vol. 22, no. 3 (March):1279–1310.

Kosowski, Robert, Allan G. Timmermann, Russ Wermers, and Hal White. 2006. "Can Mutual Fund 'Stars' Really Pick Stocks? New Evidence from a Bootstrap Analysis." *Journal of Finance*, vol. 61, no. 6 (December):2551–2595.

Kritzman, Mark. 2012. "Two Things about Performance Fees." *Journal of Portfolio Management*, vol. 38, no. 2 (Winter):4–5.

Lin, Crystal, and Kenneth Young. 2004. "Real Estate Mutual Funds: Performance and Persistence." *Journal of Real Estate Research*, vol. 26, no. 1:69–93.

Mamaysky, Harry, Matthew Spiegel, and Hong Zhang. 2008. "Estimating the Dynamics of Mutual Fund Alphas and Betas." *Review of Financial Studies*, vol. 21, no. 1 (January):233–264.

Margrabe, William. 1978. "The Value of an Option to Exchange One Asset for Another." *Journal of Finance*, vol. 33, no. 1 (March):177–186.

McCurdy, Patrick J. 2012. "Understanding Investor Due Diligence." White paper, Merlin Securities.

Miller, Chet, and Laura Cardinal. 1994. "Strategic Planning and Firm Performance: A Synthesis of More than Two Decades of Research." *Academy of Management Journal*, vol. 37, no. 6:1649–1665.

Olson, Russell. 2005. *The School of Hard Knocks: The Evolution of Pension Investing at Eastman Kodak*. Rochester, NY: RIT Cary Graphic Arts Press.

P&I. 2006. "Top U.S. Institutional Tax-Exempt Index Fund Managers." *Pensions & Investments* 2006 Databook (25 December).

Payne, John, and Arnold Wood. 2002. "Individual Decision Making and Group Decision Processes." *Journal of Psychology and Financial Markets*, vol. 3, no. 2 (June):94–101.

Piros, Christopher. 1998. "Asset Allocation: Separating Alphas and Asset Classes." Working paper, Massachusetts Financial Services (March).

PriceMetrix. 2011. "Fee and Managed Asset Pricing." *PriceMetrix Insights*, vol. 3 (March).

PRIM. 2010. "Annual Report 2010." Massachusetts Pension Reserves Investment Management Board (7 December).

Sharpe, William F. 1991. "The Arithmetic of Active Management." *Financial Analysts Journal*, vol. 47, no. 1 (January/February):7–9.

Sharpe, William, Gordon Alexander, and Jeffery Bailey. 1999. *Investments*. 6th ed. Upper Saddle River, NJ: Prentice Hall.

Shrider, David. 2009. "Running from a Bear: How Poor Stock Market Performance Affects the Determinants of Mutual Fund Flows." *Journal of Business Finance & Accounting*, vol. 36, no. 7–8 (September/October):987–1006.

Siegel, Laurence B., Kenneth F. Kroner, and Scott W. Clifford. 2001. "The Greatest Return Stories Ever Told." *Journal of Investing*, vol. 10, no. 2 (Summer):91–102.

Starks, Laura. 1987. "Performance Incentive Fees: An Agency Theoretic Approach." *Journal of Financial and Quantitative Analysis*, vol. 22, no. 1 (March):17–32.

Stewart, Scott. 1995. "The Advantage of High Yielding Equities for Taxable Corporate Investors." In *New Directions in Finance*. Edited by D. Ghosh and S. Khaksari. Florence, KY: Routledge Publishing.

———. 1998. "Is Consistency of Performance a Good Measure of Manager Skill?" *Journal of Portfolio Management*, vol. 24, no. 3 (Spring):22–32.

———. 2013. "Training Student Equity Analysts and Utilizing Their Recommendations in Active Portfolio Management." Boston University Research Series Paper 2012-17 (May).

Stewart, Scott, Jeffrey Heisler, and Christopher Piros. 2011. *Running Money: Professional Portfolio Management*. New York: McGraw-Hill.

Stewart, Scott, Jeffrey Heisler, Christopher Knittel, and John Neumann. 2009. "Absence of Value: An Analysis of Investment Allocation Decisions by Institutional Plan Sponsors." *Financial Analysts Journal*, vol. 65, no. 6 (November/December):34–51.

Stolze, William. 1999. *Start Up: An Entrepreneur's Guide to Launching and Managing a New Business*. Pompton Plains, NJ: Career Press.

Stracca, Livio. 2006. "Delegated Portfolio Management: A Survey of the Theoretical Literature." *Journal of Economic Surveys*, vol. 20, no. 5 (December):823–848.

Swensen, David F. 2000. *Pioneering Portfolio Management: An Unconventional Approach to Institutional Investment*. New York: The Free Press, Simon and Schuster.

Teo, Melvyn, and Sung-Jun Woo. 2004. "Style Effects in the Cross-Section of Stock Returns." *Journal of Financial Economics*, vol. 74, no. 2 (November):367–398.

Tkac, Paula. 2001. "The Performance of Open-End International Mutual Funds." *Economic Review (Federal Reserve Bank of Atlanta)*, vol. 86, no. 3 (Third Quarter):1–17.

Tobe, Chris. 1999. "Letter of the Law: Social Security Investing without the Politics." *Plan Sponsor* (April).

Towers Watson. 2011. "Assessing Investment Skill in Equity Managers" (September).

———. 2012. "Global Pensions Asset Study—2012" (January).

———. 2013. "Global Pensions Asset Study—2013" (January).

Treynor, Jack. 1990. "The 10 Most Important Questions to Ask in Selecting a Money Manager." *Financial Analysts Journal*, vol. 46, no. 3 (May/June):4–5.

Vangelisti, Marco. 2006. "The Capacity of an Equity Strategy." *Journal of Portfolio Management*, vol. 32, no. 2 (Winter):44–50.

Viñas, Keila, and Scott Stewart. 2012. "Is There Career Value in the CFA Designation?" Unpublished manuscript presented at the 2013 Eastern Finance Association and Financial Management Association annual meetings (April and October).

Waring, Barton, Duane Whitney, John Pirone, and Charles Castille. 2000. "Optimizing Manager Structure and Budgeting Manager Risk." *Journal of Portfolio Management*, vol. 26, no. 3 (Spring):90–104.

Wiklund, Johan, and Dean Shepherd. 2005. "Entrepreneurial Orientation and Small Business Performance: A Configurational Approach." *Journal of Business Venturing*, vol. 20, no. 1 (January):71–91.

Zagorsky, Jay. 2007. "Do You Have to Be Smart to Be Rich? The Impact of IQ on Wealth, Income and Financial Distress." *Intelligence*, vol. 35, no. 6 (September–October):489–501.

Zheng, Lu. 1999. "Is Money Smart? A Study of Mutual Fund Investors' Fund Selection Ability." *Journal of Finance*, vol. 54, no. 3 (March):901–993.